A.D. Mills is Emeritus Reader in Medieval English, University of London, and is a member of the Council of the English Place-Name Society and of the Society for Name Studies in Britain and Ireland. He has made a life-long study of the origins and meanings of English place-names, in particular those of Dorset. As the Dorset editor for the detailed Survey of English Place-Names being conducted by the English Place-Name Society, he has produced three volumes of *The Place-Names of Dorset*, with the fourth volume under preparation and soon to be published to complete the survey of the county. His other books include *The Dorset Lay Subsidy Roll of* 1332 (Dorset Record Society), *A Dictionary of London Place-Names* (Oxford University Press), *The Place-Names of the Isle of Wight* (Shaun Tyas), and *A Dictionary of British Place-Names* (Oxford University Press).

DISCOVER DORSET

PLACE-NAMES

A.D. MILLS

THE DOVECOTE PRESS

For Bethany, Hanna, Thomas, Charlotte and Oliver.

'The name Toller Porcorum is peculiar, but of remarkable names of places this Toller is by no means the only example in the county. We have, on this side of Dorset, Whitchurch Canonicorum and Ryme Intrinseca. We have also in the county the Wriggle River and the Devil's Brook, God's Blessing Green and Giddy Green, Grammar's Hill and Mount Ararat, Hungry Down and Dancing Hill. The names of certain farms and holdings are possibly more curious still. There is something of the forlorn hope about Ratcombe Barn, Wooden Cabbage Farm and Labour-in-Vain. Starvington Farm, Poor Lot, and Charity Bottom are not attractive titles for those who have property to sell. Botany Bay Barn and Menagerie have no doubt a story, while there is the sarcasm of utter isolation about Bedlam, Marshalsea, and Bridewell.'

Frederick Treves, *Highways and Byways in Dorset,* 1906

This new revised edition first published in 2008 by
The Dovecote Press Ltd
Stanbridge, Wimborne Minster, Dorset BH21 4JD

ISBN 978-1-904-34962-4

Typeset in Palatino
Printed and bound by Baskerville Press, Salisbury, Wiltshire

All papers used by The Dovecote Press
are natural, recyclable products made from
wood grown in sustainable, well-managed forests

A CIP catalogue record for this book is available
from the British Library

CONTENTS

INTRODUCTION

There is a perennial fascination about the origins and meanings of place-names, those familiar but often curious labels for places, not least in a county like Dorset which is blessed with such a rich variety of them. This book sets out to provide all those who know Dorset, whether fortunate enough to live in the county or only passing through, with information about the origins of its place-names, their history, their underlying meaning and their significance.

The alphabetical list of Dorset place-names includes most of the names to be found on the 1:50000 series of maps published by the Ordnance Survey. It provides the basic information about the history and origin of each name, as far as it is known: (*a*) its modern form as it appears on map or signpost; (*b*) some representative early spellings for the name, with dates, to show how the name has developed; (*c*) the probable original meaning of the name, deduced from those early spellings; (*d*) the elements (i.e. words) or personal names from which the name is derived; (*e*) other brief comments where appropriate on points of linguistic, geographical or historical significance.

THE IMPORTANCE OF EARLY SPELLINGS

Most place-names today are, as it were, linguistic fossils. Although they began life as living units of speech - as descriptions, in a living language, of places in terms of their topography, appearance, situation, use, ownership, or other association - most have become, in the course of time, mere labels, no longer possessing a clear linguistic meaning. It is only by tracing each name back to its earliest spelling in the records that its original meaning can be discovered and its original significance appreciated.

Of course some place-names, even very old ones, have changed very little through the many centuries of their existence. Dorset names like Okeford, Sandford and Thornford are still self-explanatory, even though they are several hundred years old and though the fords themselves from which the places took their names may long since have been replaced by bridges. Similarly, old names like Blackmoor, Marshwood and Woodbridge are shown by their early spellings to have had original meanings that still seem obvious today.

But even a casual glance at the alphabetical list of Dorset place-names will show that such instant etymologies are often a delusion. The modern form of a name can never be *assumed* to convey its original meaning without early spellings to confirm it. We find, for instance, that Wool has nothing to do with sheep, that Beer has no brewery, and that Kingcombe has no royal associations! Apparently identical names can have quite different etymologies. Thus Hinton St Mary differs in origin from Hinton Martell, likewise Burton Bradstock from Long Burton. Of the two pairs of places called Orchard, one pair has the obvious meaning 'orchard', virtually unchanged through nine centuries, whereas the other pair has an even older Celtic name, now disguised, as it were, through changes in spelling. All three of the Dorset places called Holwell have quite different origins, as have the two places called Gummershay.

Dorset has its share of place-names, some of them very old, that are to be found in several other English counties. Names like Kingston, Knighton, Charlton, Buckland and Sherborne occur elsewhere in England, and their origins are usually straightforward. However, here too the early spellings are crucial for correct interpretation. Dorset names that are apparently identical with names in other counties often turn out to be quite different in origin. The Dorset Acton could look as if it might be the common 'oak-tree farm', but early spellings show otherwise. Similarly, Dorchester and Gillingham both have different origins from their namesakes in Oxfordshire and Kent.

A good many Dorset place-names are unique to the county, often containing rare old words found in very few other English names and usually now obsolete. These include Blashenwell, Blandford, Gussage, Spetisbury, Tincleton, Worgret and many others. Early spellings do not always provide a clear unambiguous etymology, hence the large number of names for which alternative, or only tentative, explanations are suggested. In some names, such as Chelborough, Pamphill and Shaftesbury, the first element could be either a significant word or a personal name.

Not all the place-names can be satisfactorily explained, even in terms of alternative possibilities. A few names, like Caundle, Chickerell and Powerstock, remain for the time being at least partly obscure, even though early spellings are available. On the other hand, there are a few names, such as Ballard Down, Durlston and Sugar Hill, for which a tentative etymology may be proposed, on the basis of analogy with similar names elsewhere, even though no early spellings are recorded.

Most of the Dorset place-names so far mentioned (except for Dorchester and one of the pairs called Orchard) are of Old English or Anglo-Saxon origin. This is the dominant stratum in the place-names of Dorset, as in other English counties apart from Cornwall, and is the legacy of the Germanic peoples, the Anglo-Saxons, who first came to Britain from about the fifth century AD, and who were settling in Dorset from the seventh century onwards. Thus the majority of Dorset towns and villages, and a good many hamlets, farms and landscape features, have names that were first coined in the language of the Anglo-Saxons, that is in Old English, between the seventh and eleventh centuries. Dorset of course was within the old kingdom of Wessex, that is within the area settled by the West Saxons, and many Dorset place-names, such as Chaldon, Marnhull, Shapwick and Wool, reflect the distinctive West Saxon dialect spoken in this region.

The names of Old English origin vary in age, but it is not always easy to tell which names belong to the earlier and which to the later part of the period. What is certain, however, is that names recorded in Domesday Book (compiled in 1086) or earlier, apart from the Celtic names mentioned in the next paragraph, will have had their origins in the Old English period. In fact many other names too, first on record in later medieval documents, may well have been coined in Old English times, since the date of the earliest occurrence of a name in a surviving manuscript is largely a matter of chance.

However, the oldest place-names in Dorset are those of British or Celtic origin. Such Celtic names as have survived are relatively few in number, but they are particularly interesting because they provide evidence of continuity and contact between the Celtic-speaking Britons and their English-speaking conquerors, the West Saxons. In fact the conquered Britons must have passed these names on during the Anglo-Saxon occupation of Dorset in the seventh century, so most of them are probably a good deal older than that (the original Celtic names for Dorchester and Badbury are recorded as early as the fourth century). Most of the surviving Celtic names are names of rivers or other natural features, although these have often been later transferred to settlements. They include river-names like Cerne, Char, Lim, Lydden, Tarrant, Trent and Wey, original stream-names like Fontmell, Winfrith and Wynford, hill-names like Creech, Crichel, Crook, Pen and Pentridge, and wood-names like Chideock, Lytchett and the Orchard already mentioned.

Only a few names in Dorset, as in most other English counties, are French in origin, in spite of the far-reaching effects of the Norman conquest on the English language in general. It is clear that by 1066, most settlements and landscape features already had established names, and the new Norman aristocracy only rarely gave French names to parts of their estates (Organ Ford may be an example of a name actually transferred from France). But the influence of this powerful French-speaking aristocracy is revealed in the way the names of the great feudal families were affixed to the names of the manors they possessed. These manorial additions result in a great many hybrid double-barrelled names which contribute considerable variety and richness to the map of Dorset. Most of these additions serve to distinguish one manor from another with an identical name, either in Dorset or some other county, like Langton Herring and Matravers, Fifehead Neville and St Quintin, Bradford Peverell, and Kingston Lacy. Some of the important Norman families are represented in more than one name, as in Okeford and Wootton Fitzpaine, Langton and Worth Matravers. Many of the manorial additions are now compounded with the original name itself, as in Hammoon, Owermoigne, and Stourpaine. The Norman-French influence also shows itself in rather different ways in a few other names like Corfe Mullen, Font le Roi, La Lee and Piddletrenthide. Beaulieu, however, although it now looks like a French name, is a refashioning of a purely English one.

Mention must also be made of the interesting presence of Latin among the place-names of Dorset. There are no names of purely Latin origin, but quite a number of names which have had a Latin affix added in medieval times. This reflects the widespread use of Latin by church and state - it was the language most often used by scribes in medieval documents relating to law and administration. Presumably so many of the Latin additions survive because they became fixed and accepted in writing, even though one suspects they may never have been used very much in popular speech. Many of them give an indication of ownership, as by the king (Bere Regis, Melcombe Regis), an abbey (Bradford Abbas, Compton Abbas) or other religious foundation (Whitchurch Canonicorum). Some allude to administrative arrangements (Ryme Intrinseca) or relative size (Kington Magna). Others are used to distinguish two manors with identical names, like Fontmell Magna and Parva or Toller Fratrum and Porcorum ('of the brethren' and 'of the pigs' - there is surely a medieval joke here, and one wonders who was being got at!).

Of course, not all the names on the modern map, even names of sizeable settlements, are as old as most of those so far mentioned. Many names for smaller settlements, farmsteads and topographical features probably originate in the Middle English period, that is from the twelfth to the fifteenth century inclusive. Names such as Bailey Ridge, Eastbury, Forston, Hermitage and Lenthay belong here. Others, like Burning Cliff and Decoy Heath, date only from the nineteenth century, as do transferred names like Botany and Waterloo. Relatively few names are of recent creation, but Northbourne, Southbourne, Springbourne and Westbourne for the modern districts of Bournemouth are examples.

FOLK ETYMOLOGY, BACK-FORMATION AND EUPHEMISM

Once the original meaning of an old place-name has been obscured or lost - because words have gone out of use, or because the person commemorated has been forgotten, or because of changes in pronunciation and spelling - there is often a tendency for a process of rationalization or reinterpretation to take place, a process sometimes known as folk etymology. Numerous Dorset place-names show the process at work. They include Devil's Brook, Goathorn, Hengistbury, Sixpenny Handley, Slaughtergate, Wadmill and Wolfridge. In all these names, familiar words, quite unhistorical but making a kind of sense, have been substituted for unfamiliar or obscure words.

Folk etymology sometimes results in a phenomenon known as back-formation. This is especially common in the creation of river-names in comparatively recent times. Thus Crane came to be the name of the river at Cranborne because the village name (historically 'crane stream, stream frequented by cranes') came to be understood as 'stream called Crane'. Other examples of back-formation include the river-names Allen, Asker, Mude and Simene.

Euphemism, the tendency to replace an offensive name by one that sounds less so, has also played its part in the history of some names. The names Arish Mell and Merritown may be instances. The medieval bluntness of Arish Mell contrasts with the relative coyness in recent times noted under Puddletown and Shitterton.

PLACE-NAMES AND THE LANDSCAPE

Obviously the place-names of Dorset relate very closely to the landscape they describe, a landscape seen through the eyes of the earlier inhabitants of the county. The importance of river valleys for early settlement - providing fertile soils and a water supply - is reflected in the number of Dorset places named from the rivers on which they are situated. The two rivers called Winterborne provide the names of over a dozen places, all distinguished one from another by additions. Similarly the River Tarrant gives its name to no less than eight different places, the River Piddle to six, the Rivers Frome and Wey to four each, and so on. Many other places are named from the quite small streams on which they stand, like Trent, Trill and Iwerne. The numerous places that take their names from fords, like Blandford and Canford, show the early importance of river crossings. Other topographical features - hills and valleys, moors and marshes, springs and pools, estuaries and promontories - are well represented among the names. The wide range and variety of this topographical vocabulary is to be noted. Many names indicate woodland, or clearings in woodland, clearly reflecting a period when wooded areas were much more extensive than they are today. Natural history is also well represented among the place-names of Dorset. Many different species of trees and plants, wild animals and birds, fish and even insects are evidenced.

PLACE-NAMES AND HUMAN ACTIVITY

Dorset place-names also reflect the many and various aspects of human activity in the area during the different phases of its history. Many names refer to particular kinds of early habitation and settlement sites, others have important archaeological implications or significant religious associations. Many more provide information about the agricultural economy of earlier times, with their references to man-made enclosures, arable land, meadows, pastures and orchards. Some names refer to the kind or quality of the soil, others to the livestock raised, others to the crops produced. Several names contain elements that suggest the importance of communication and trade in early times. Others reflect the importance of local industries and occupations, from milling and fishing to salt-making, charcoal-burning, pot-making, hunting and quarrying.

Many persons and families from many different periods of history are commemorated in the place-names of Dorset. Some of the Anglo-Saxon men and women who bore Old English names may have been among the settlers who colonized Dorset from the seventh century onwards, like the Gylla who gave name to Gillingham, but most of them occupied their estates at a somewhat later date. About many of them, like the Cana who gave name to Canford (and possibly to Canon

Hill), nothing more is known, and even some of their personal names are hypothetical. Others, like the Here who gave name to Herston and the Beorn of Barnston are actually on record as known individuals. Quite a number of these early manorial landowners were women, like the Ælfrun of Afflington and the Tola of Tolpuddle. However, it should be noted that some Old English personal names, like the Betti of Bettiscombe and the Ella of Elworth, are names of men even though they may resemble more recent women's names.

Besides such individuals, known and unknown, many families are likewise recalled in the place-names. As already noted, the great landowning families, often of Norman French descent, have left their mark on Dorset place-names in the manorial additions of names like Kingston Lacy, Fifehead Neville and Langton Matravers. Most of these families were influential and well documented. Others, like the families that gave name to places like Cruxton, Silkhay, Bluntshay and Moorcourt, were often rather less notable and only known in local records.

FOLKLORE AND SPECIAL ALLUSIONS

Some Dorset place-names, like Agglestone, Crab Farm, Elwell and Fortuneswell, are to be associated with popular beliefs and superstitions. Others refer to heathen gods (Grim's Ditch) or contain references to goblins (Puckstone, and possibly Pokedown) or to the devil (Old Harry). Motcombe refers to an old assembly place, and Pistle Down is an allusion to the ceremony of beating the bounds at Rogationtide. A few names are grim reminders of the violent punishments meted out to criminals in earlier times (Gallows Hill, Worgret, Yewstock). Some allude to sports and pastimes (Landscombe Lane, Merry Field Hill, Miz Maze, Troy Town). In some the precise nature of the allusion is uncertain, since it may be figurative or ironical (Giddy Green, Gaulter Gap, Harp Stone, Stapehill, Three Legged Cross). A few names are transferred from other places outside England, and here too the exact significance is not always clear (Mount Ararat, Normandy, Waterloo). Others contain literary allusions (Branksome, Lilliput) or commemorate a historical event (Monmouth's Ash).

The introduction has only touched upon a few of the points of interest arising from a study of the place-names of Dorset. The alphabetical list of the names will provide a lot more information, but those seeking a more detailed coverage of the place-names (and field-names) of Dorset, together with a fuller discussion and analysis, should consult the series of county volumes published by the English Place-Name Society.

ALPHABETICAL LIST

Abbeycroft Down (in Tarrant Rushton) *Abbey Croft* 1542. From Old English *croft* 'enclosure'. It belonged to Tarrant Abbey.

Abbey House (in Witchampton) called *The Abbey Barn* in the 18th century, but by tradition once a chapel.

Abbotsbury *Abbedesburie* 946 (later copy of Saxon charter), *Abedesberie* 1086 (Domesday Book), *Abbodesberia* 1194. 'Fortified house or manor of the abbot', from Old English *abbod* and *burh*, referring to the abbot of Glastonbury who held lands here at an early date; the monastery at Abbotsbury itself was not founded until c.1026.

Abbot's Court Farm (in Winterborne Kingston) *Abescourte* 1553. 'Court or manor house of the abbess', from Middle English *abbesse* and *court*, alluding to the abbess of Tarrant who held lands here from the 13th century. The modern name is thus rather misleading.

Abbott Street (in Pamphill) *Abbodestrete* 1340. 'Abbot's hamlet', referring to possession of the manor by the Abbey of Sherborne.

Abbott's Wootton Farms (in Whitchurch Canonicorum) *Wudetune* 1044 (Saxon charter), *Widetone* 1086 (Domesday Book), *Wodeton Abbatis* 1268. 'Farm in or by a wood', from Old English *wudu* and *tūn*. Latin *abbatis* 'of the abbot' refers to early possession by Abbotsbury Abbey.

Acton (in Langton Matravers) *Tacatone* 1086 (Domesday Book), *Tacton* 1283. Probably 'farm where young sheep are reared', from Old English *tacca* and *tūn*. The original T- was only dropped in 16th century.

Adber (in Trent) *Eatan beares* 956 (12th century copy of Saxon charter), *Ateberie, Ettebere* 1086 (Domesday Book). 'Grove of a man called Ēata', from an Old English personal name and *bearu*.

Admiston, South (in Athelhampton) a variant of Athelhampton.

Afflington Farm (in Corfe Castle) *Alvronetone, Alfrunetone* 1086 (Domesday Book), *Alfrington* 1244. 'Farm or estate of a lady called Ælfrūn', from an Old English personal name and *tūn*. This woman held the manor at the time of Domesday Book.

Affpuddle *Affapidele* 1086 (Domesday Book), *Affepidel* 1244. 'Estate on River Piddle of a man called Æffa', from an Old English personal name.

Agglestone (in Studland) *Adlingston* 1586. 'Prince's stone', from Old English *ætheling* and *stān*. According to folklore, this massive block of sandstone was thrown by the Devil from the Isle of Wight with the intention of demolishing Corfe Castle!

Ailwood (in Corfe Castle) *Aleoude* 1086 (Domesday Book), *Ailewud* 1222. 'Wood of a woman called Æthelgifu', from an Old English personal name and *wudu*.

Alcester (in Shaftesbury) *Alcestre* 1433. This name was transferred from Alcester in Warwickshire, since Alcester Abbey possessed lands here from at least as early as the 13th century.

Alderholt *Alreholt* 1285, *Halreholt* 1328. 'Alder wood', from Old English *alor* and *holt*.

Alders Coppice (in Shillingstone) *Alres* 1330. Old English *alor*.

Allen, River originally called *Wimborne,* a name transferred to Wimborne Minster and St Giles. Its present name is taken from the bridge at Wimborne Minster now called Canford Bridge but earlier *Aldewynebrigg* 1268, 'bridge of a man called Ealdwine', from an Old English personal name and *brycg*.

Aller (in Hilton) *Alre* 1332. From Old English *alor* 'an alder' .

All Hallows Farm (in Wimborne St Giles) *Opewinburne* 1086 (Domesday Book), *Vpwymburne All Saints* 1294, *Alhalowes Wimborn* 1575. For *Vpwymburne,* see Wimborne St Giles. All Hallows (from Old English *hālga* 'saint') is from the dedication of the former church here. In medieval times sometimes called *Wymborn Karentham* (as in 1291) from a family of that name.

Allington *Adelingtone* 1086 (Domesday Book), *Athelington* 1227. 'Farm or estate of the princes', from Old English *ætheling* and *tūn*.

Allweston (in Folke) *Alfeston, Alveston* 1214, *Alfletheston* 1244, *Alueueston* 1268. 'Farm of a man called Ælf', from Old English personal name and *tūn*. Or 'stone of a woman called Ælfflæd or Ælfgifu', from Old English personal name and *stān*.

Almer (in Sturminster Marshall) *Elmere* 943 (15th century copy of Saxon charter), *Almere* 1212. 'Eel pool', from Old English *æl* and *mere,* with reference to the pool just south-east of the village.

Alton Pancras *Awultune* 1012, *Altone* 1086 (Domesday Book), *Aweltone Pancratii* 1226. 'Farm at the source of a stream', from Old English *æwiell* and *tūn;* the River Piddle rises here. Addition Pancras (Latin *Pancratius)* is from the dedication of the church.

Alum Chine (in Bournemouth) first recorded in the 18th century, presumably an allusion to the earlier mining of alum here. Chine is from an Old English word *cinu* 'a deep valley, a ravine'.

Amen Corner (in Gussage All Saints) recorded thus in 1869, according to tradition once the site of a chapel.

Ameysford (in Hampreston) first recorded 1791, probably named from a family called *Amey*. The ford was across Uddens Water.

Anderson *Wintreburne* 1086 (Domesday Book), *Wynterborn Fifasse* 1268, *Andreweston* 1331. Originally named from River Winterborne. The addition *Fifasse* means 'five ash-trees', from Old English *fíf* and *æsc*. The later *Andreweston* which forms the basis of the present name is probably from the dedication of the disused St Andrew's Church, with Old English *tūn* 'estate' .

Angers Farm (in Okeford Fitzpaine) *Aungiers* 1601. Named from a family called *Aunger*, here from the 14th century.

Ansty (in Hilton) *Anesty* 1219, *Ansty* 1244. 'Narrow track, or track linking other routes', from Old English *ānstīg*.

Arish Mell (in East Lulworth) *Arsmyll* 1454, *Arish Mill* 1634. 'The mill near a topographical feature resembling a buttock', from Old English *ears* and *myln*. Our forefathers were not coy in using terms for parts of the body to describe their surroundings!

Armswell Farm (in Piddletrenthide) *Ermingewell* 1225, *Ermingyswelle* 1303. Probably 'spring or stream of a man called Eormen', from an Old English personal name and *wella*.

Arne *Arne* 1268, *Harne* 1285, *Arn* 1327, *Aren* 1575. Probably 'the house or building', from Old English *ærn*, or '(place at) the heaps of stones or tumuli', from Old English *hær* (dative plural *harum*).

Ash, '(place at) the ash-tree(s)', from Old English *æsc*: (i) **Ash** (in Netherbury) *Esse* 1207, *Ashe* 1316. (ii) **Ash** (in Stourpaine) *Aisse* 1086 (Domesday Book), *Esse* 1244, *Assche* 1280.

Ashcombe Farm (in Caundle Marsh) *Ascumbe* 1205. 'Valley where ash-trees grow', from Old English *æsc* and *cumb*.

Ashington (in Canford Magna) *Esseton* 1243, *Ashamton* 1327. Probably 'farm of the dwellers by the ash-tree(s)', from Old English *æsc*, *hæme* and *tūn*.

Ashley, 'ash-tree wood or clearing', from Old English *æsc* and *lēah*: (i) **Ashley** (in Long Bredy) *Asseleghe* 1246. (ii) **Ashley** (in St Leonards and St Ives) *Aisshele* 1280. (iii) **Ashley Barn** (in Tolpuddle) *Asleg* 1268. (iv) **Ashley Wood** (in Tarrant Keynston) *Ashelie Wood* 1624.

Ashmore *Aisemare* 1086 (Domesday Book), *Assemere* 1235, *Aysschemere* 1283. 'Pool where ash-trees grow', Old English *æsc* and *mere*, referring to the pond at the centre of this hill-top village.

Ashton Farm (in Hinton Parva) *Esseton* 1243, *Ashton* 1841. 'Farm by the ash-tree(s)', from Old English *æsc* and *tūn*.

Ashton Farm (in Winterborne St Martin) *Wintreburne* 1086 (Domesday Book), *Winterburn Asshe* 1275, *Aschtone* 1327. Originally named from the South Winterborne River on which it stands, later with Old English *æsc* 'ash-tree' and *tūn* 'farm, estate'.

Asker, River a late back-formation from Askerswell.

Askerswell *Oscherwille* 1086 (Domesday Book), *Oskereswell* 1201. 'Spring or stream of a man called Ōsgār', from an Old English personal name and *wella*.

Athelhampton *Pidele* 1086 (Domesday Book), *Pidele Aleume* 1250, *(Pidele) Athelamston* 1285, *Athelhameston* 1303. Originally named from River Piddle on which it stands, but later 'farm of a man called Æthelhelm', from Old English personal name and *tūn*.

Atrim (in Netherbury) *Atrem, Atrum* 1086 (Domesday Book). Possibly the old name for River Simene, but its origin is obscure.

Attisham (in Broadwindsor) *Adesham* 1252. 'Enclosure of a man called Æddi', from an Old English personal name and *hamm*.

Axe Farm (in Broadwindsor) *Axe* 1252. Named from River Axe on which it stands. Axe is an old Celtic river-name meaning 'water'; it also gives its name to Axminster and Axmouth in Devon.

Axnoller Farms (in Beaminster) *Axnolre* 1285. 'Alder-tree(s) by River Axe', Old English *alor*. For the river-name, see Axe Farm.

Badbury Rings (in Shapwick) this Iron Age hill-fort was called *Vindocladia* in the 4th century, an old Celtic name meaning '(the town with) the white ditches', from *uindo-* and *clādo-*, clearly a reference to the chalk of which the hill-fort is constructed. The present name is *Baddan byrig* in the 10th century (Anglo-Saxon Chronicle), 'fortification of a man called Badda', from an Old English personal name (perhaps that of a legendary hero) and *burh*.

Bagber (in Sturminster Newton) *Bakeberge* 1201, *Bakebere* 1204. Probably 'hill or grove of a man called Bacca', from an Old English personal name with *beorg* or *bearu*.

Bagman's Farm (in Woodlands) *Bagerham* (probably an error for *Bagenham*) 1237, *Baggeham* 1305. Probably Old English *bagga* 'bag', either as a topographical word for a hill or as the name of an animal, possibly the badger, with Old English *hamm* 'enclosure'.

Bailey Ridge Farm (in Lillington) *La Baillie* 1351, *Baylyrygge* 1496. From Middle English *baillie* 'a bailiff's district', and *hrycg* 'ridge'.

Bailie Gate (in Sturminster Marshall) *Baylye Yeate* 1516. 'The gate of a bailiwick or bailiff's district', from Middle English *baillie* and Old English *geat*. The bailiff may have had charge of a stretch of woodland or of the river-bank of the Stour.

Bainly Farm (in Gillingham) *Binley* 1609. 'Clearing where beans are grown', from Old English *bēan* and *lēah*.

Ballard Down and Point (in Studland) not on record until 1811, but probably 'rounded headland', Old English *balg* and *hēafod*.

Baltington (in Tyneham) *Boltington* 1280, *Baltington* 1284. Probably 'farm called after a man named Beald', from an Old English personal name and *-ingtūn*.

Barcombe Farm (in Alton Pancras) *Berecombe* 1332. Probably 'valley where barley is grown', from Old English *bere* and *cumb*.

Bardolf Manor and Basan Hill (in Puddletown) *Pidelebardolveston* 1257, *Pidel Bardolf* 1264. 'Estate on River Piddle of the *Bardolf* family', from Old English *tūn*. This family was here in the 13th century. Basan is a much reduced form of *Bardolveston*.

Barford Farm (in Pamphill) *Bereford* 1244. 'Ford by the woodland pasture or grove', Old English *bær* or *bearu* and *ford*.

Barnsfield Heath (near Hurn) *Barndefeld* early 12th century. 'Tract of land cleared by burning', Old English *berned* and *feld*.

Barnsley Farm (in Pamphill) *Bernardeslega* 1178. 'Woodland clearing of a man called Beornheard', Old English personal name and *lēah*.

Barnston Farm (in Church Knowle) *Berneston* 1288. 'Farm of a man called Beorn', from Old English personal name and *tūn*. The man in question held lands here at the time of Domesday Book.

Barton Hill (in Shaftesbury) named from the manor of *Berton* 1288, Old English *bere-tūn* 'a corn farm, an outlying grange'.

Basan Hill (in Puddletown) see Bardolf Manor.

Batcombe *Batecumbe* 1201. Probably 'valley of a man called Bata', from an Old English personal name and *cumb*.

Bay (in Gillingham) first recorded 1791, probably from the word *bay* 'an embankment to form a dam'.

Beacon Hill (in Lytchett Minster) from *Lechiot becon* 1575.

Beaminster *Bebingmynster* 862 (14th century copy of Saxon charter), *Beiminstre* 1086 (Domesday Book), *Begminister* 1091. 'Church of a woman called Bēage', from an Old English personal name and *mynster*. She perhaps founded or endowed the church.

Bearwood (in Canford Magna) from 1840, same origin as Beer(e).

Beaulieu Wood (in Buckland Newton) *Beleye* 1288. 'Wood or clearing frequented by bees', from Old English *bēo* and *lēah*.

Bedchester (in Fontmell Magna) *Bedeshurste* early 12th century, *Bedcester* 1576. 'Wooded hill of a man called Bēdi or Bæde', from an Old English personal name and *hyrst*. See Hogchester.

Beere Farm (in Thorncombe) *La Bere* 1281. Probably from Old English *bearu* 'a wood, a grove'.

Beer Hackett *Bera* 1176, *Berehaket* 1362. 'The woodland pasture' or 'the grove', from Old English *bær* or *bearu*. Manorial addition from *Haket de Bera* who held the manor from 1176.

Beerhall Farm (in Thorncombe) *Berehalle* 1377. 'Hall or manor house by the grove', from Old English *bearu* and *hall*.

Belchalwell (in Okeford Fitzpaine) *Chaldewelle* 1109, *Bell* 1207, *Belle and Chaldwell* 1286, *Belchalwell* 1575. Originally two distinct names. *Chaldwell* is 'cold spring or stream', from Old English *ceald* and *wella; Belle* is from Old English *belle* 'bell-shaped hill', referring to Bell Hill (845 feet).

Belhuish Farm (in West Lulworth) *Behylde Hywysche* 1303, *Belhywyssh* 1331. 'Measure of land of a woman called Bēaghild', from an Old English personal name and *hīwisc*.

Bellows Cross (in Cranborne) *Bellyes Crosse* 1621, named from *Belleye* 1382, probably 'clearing at the bell-shaped hill', from Old English *belle* and *lēah*.

Benville Manor (in Corscombe) *Benefeld* 1340. 'Arable land where beans are grown', from Old English *bēan* and *feld*.

Bere Farm (in Lytchett Minster) *Bearecourt* 1374, *Bere* 1420. Has the same origin as Bere Regis, with the addition of Middle English *court* 'manor house' up to 16th century.

Bere Marsh Farm and Mill (in Shillingstone) *molendinum* ('mill') *de la Bere* 1268, *Berre marshe* 1546. Probably from Old English *bær* '(woodland) pasture'. The place is by River Stour.

Bere Regis *Bere* 1086 (Domesday Book), *Kyngesbyre* 1264, *Bire Regis* 1495. 'Woodland pasture', or 'wood, grove', from Old English *bær* or *bearu*. This was a royal manor attached to a royal forest, hence the Latin addition *Regis* 'of the king'.

Berne Farm (in Whitchurch Canonicorum) *La Berne* 1281. 'The barn, or storehouse for grain', from Old English *bere-ærn*.

Berry Hill (in Bournemouth) possibly to be associated with *la Bury* 13th century, from Old English *burh* 'a fortified place'.

Berwick (in Swyre) *Berewich* 1194, *Berewyk* 1250. Old English *bere-wīc* 'barley-farm', often also 'outlying part of an estate'.

Bestwall (in Wareham) *Beastewelle* 1086 (Domesday Book), *Biestewalle* 1293. '(Place) to the east of the wall', from Old English *bī* 'by, near', *ēastan* and *weall*.

Bettiscombe *Bethescomme* 1129, *Betescumbe* 1244. 'Valley of a man called

Betti', from an Old English personal name and *cumb*.

Bexington (in Puncknowle) *Bessintone* 1086 (Domesday Book), *Buxinton* 1212. 'Farm where box-trees grow', from Old English *byxen* and *tūn*.

Bhompston (in Stinsford) *Frome* 1086 (Domesday Book), *Frome Bonevileston* 1285. 'Manor on River Frome of the *Boneville* family', from Old English *tūn*. They were here from 13th century.

Bibbern Farm (in Stalbridge) *Bydeburnan* 933 (12th century copy of Saxon charter), *Biddeburn* 1244. 'Stream in a hollow', from Old English *byden* and *burna*. The stream is now called Bibbern Brook.

Bidcombe Mill (in Gussage All Saints) probably named from *Bitcombe* 1327, 'valley of a man called Bitta', from an Old English personal name and *cumb*.

Biddlesgate Farm (in Cranborne) *bi talayate* 946 (14th century copy of Saxon charter), *Butelesheite* 1236. Probably 'gate of a man called Butel', from an Old English personal name and *geat*. It is on the county boundary where a road from Hampshire enters Dorset.

Bidlake Farm (in Netherbury) *Bitelak* 1225. 'Stream of a man called Bitta', from an Old English personal name and *lacu*.

Bilshay Farm (in Allington) *Bilesheye* 1244. 'Enclosure of a man called Bil', from an Old English personal name and *hæg*.

Bincombe *Beuncumbe* 987 (13th century copy of Saxon charter), *Beincome* 1086 (Domesday Book), *Benecumbe* 1288. Probably 'valley where beans are grown', from Old English *bēan* and *cumb*.

Bindon Hill, Little Bindon (in West Lulworth) *Binedon, Old Bynedon* 1279, *Litle Bindon* 1535. '(The place) within the hill', from Old English *binnan* and *dūn*. This was the site of Bindon Abbey before it was transferred to Wool in 1172. It was called *Little* or *Old* to distinguish it from Bindon Abbey itself.

Bingham's Farm (in Netherbury) originally called *Woth* in 1207, *Bynghams Wothe* in 1448. *Woth* is the earlier name of River Brit, see Wooth Grange also in this parish. An estate on this river was held by the *Bingham* family from the 13th century.

Bingham's Melcombe (in Melcombe Horsey) *Mel(e)come* 1086 (Domesday Book), *Bynghammes Melcombe* 1412. See Melcombe Horsey. Manorial addition from the *Bingham* family, here in 13th century. In early times also *Nethermelcombe* 'lower Melcombe'.

Binnegar (in East Stoke) *Beningere* 1299, *Benegar* 1318. Possibly 'slope where beans grow', from Old English *bēan* and *hangra*.

Birdsmoor Gate (in Broadwindsor) *Birds moore* 1663, from a surname.

Bishop's Down (in Folke) *Doune* 1332, *Bysshopysdoune* 1468. 'Hill or down of the bishop (of Salisbury)', from Old English *dūn*.

Bittles Green (in Motcombe) *Biddles Greene* 1609. From the family of John *le Budel* 1327.

Blackdown Hill (in Broadwindsor) *Blakedon* 1275. 'Dark-coloured hill', from Old English *blæc* and *dūn*, see Blagdon Hill.

Blackmanston Farm (in Steeple) *Blachemanestone* 1086 (Domesday Book), *Blakmanton* 1288. 'Farm of a man called Blæcmann', from an Old English personal name and *tūn*.

Blackmoor Forest and Vale *Blakemor* 1212, *Blakamor* 1239. 'Dark-coloured moor', from Old English *blæc* and *mōr*.

Blackney Farm (in Stoke Abbott) *Blakenhey* 1327. 'Dark-coloured enclosure', Old English *blæc* (dative *blacan*) and *hæg*.

Blackrow Common (in Lydlynch) *Blakerewe* 1421. 'Dark-coloured row (of trees or houses)', Old English *blæc* and *ræw*.

Blackven Common (in Fontmell Magna) *Blakkefennysmersche* 1395, *Blakevenne* 1450. '(Marsh at) the dark-coloured fen', from Old English *blæc* and *fenn* with *mersc*.

Black Venn (in East Stour) *la Blakeuenne* 13th century. 'The dark-coloured fen', from Old English *blæc* and *fenn*.

Blackwater (near Hurn) thus in 18th century, perhaps originally an earlier name for the Moors River, with *black* 'dark-coloured'.

Blagdon Farm and Hill (in Cranborne) *Blakedone* 1237. 'Dark-coloured hill', from Old English *blæc* and *dūn*. The hill reaches 529 feet and lies on the county boundary.

Blagdon Hill (in Broadwindsor) *Blakedon* 1324. Identical in origin with Blackdown Hill in the same parish.

Blandford Forum *Blaneford* 1086 (Domesday Book), *Cheping Blaneford* 1288, *Blaneford Forum* 1297. Possibly 'ford where blay or gudgeon (small freshwater fish) are found', from Old English *blæge* and *ford*. Latin *forum* (alternating with Old English *cēping*) 'market' allude to early importance of Blandford as a market town.

Blandford St Mary *Bleneford, Blaneforde* 1086 (Domesday Book), *Blaneford St Mary* 1254. For the origin of Blandford, see Blandford Forum. *St Mary* from the dedication of the church or because the manor once belonged to the nunnery of St Mary at Clerkenwell in London. In medieval times sometimes *Parva Blaneford* (Latin *parva* 'small') or *Blaneford Martel* (from a family called *Martel* which possessed the manor in the 12th century).

Blashenwell Farm (in Corfe Castle) *Blechenenwelle* 956 (14th century copy of Saxon charter). 'Spring or stream where cloth is bleached', from Old English *blæcen* 'bleaching' and *wella*, referring either to the calcareous spring near the farm or to the stream here.

Bleet Farm (in Gillingham) possibly dialect *bleat* 'cold, bleak'.

Bloxworth *Blacewyrthe* 987 (13th century copy of Saxon charter), *Blocheshorde* 1086 (Domesday Book), *Blokeswurthe* 1201. 'Enclosure of a man called Blocc', from an Old English personal name and *worth*.

Bluntshay (in Whitchurch Canonicorum) *Blondelesheye* 1312. 'Enclosure of a family called Blundel', from Old English *hæg*.

Bluntsmoor Farm (in Mosterton) called *Blountescourte* in 1486, named from the *Blunt* or *Blount* family, here from 13th century.

Blynfield Farm (in Cann) *Blinchesfelde* 932 (15th century copy of Saxon charter), *Blinchefeld* 1244. Probably 'tract of open land by the shining stream', from Old English *blinc* and *feld*.

Bockhampton (in Stinsford) *Bochehamtone* 1086 (Domesday Book), *Bocameton* 1212. Probably 'farm of the dwellers by the beech-tree', from Old English *bōc*, *hǽme* and *tūn*.

Bockhampton, Middle, North and South (in Christchurch) *Bachamton* 1199, *Bochamton* 1295. 'Beech-tree homestead', from Old English *bōc* and *hām-tūn*, or from Old English *bæc* 'a ridge'.

Bokerly Ditch (in Pentridge) *Bockedic* 1280. 'Ditch where bucks are seen', from Old English *bucc* and *dīc*, an allusion to hunting in Cranborne Chase. The ditch itself, which crosses four miles of downland, is of Romano-British origin (late 4th century).

Bonscombe (in Shipton Gorge) *Bonescumb* 13th century. From Old English *cumb* 'valley'. The first element is probably a surname; there is record of a William *Boun* here in 1332.

Bonsley Common (in Shillingstone) *Bowslye Common* 1583, *Bonslate* 1774. Perhaps from the Old English personal name *Buna* with Old English *slæget* or *slege* 'sheep pasture'.

Bookham (in Buckland Newton) *Bobbecombe* 14th century. 'Valley of a man called Bubba', from an Old English personal name and *cumb*.

Boscombe (in Bournemouth) *Boscumbe* 1273. Possibly 'valley overgrown with spiky plants', from Old English *bors* and *cumb*.

Botany Farm (in East Lulworth) *Botany* 1841, a transferred name from Botany Bay in Australia, usually denoting a remote spot.

Bothenhampton *Bothenamtone* 1285, *Baunton* 1497. 'Home farm by the valley bottom', from Old English *bothm* and *hām-tūn*.

Bothenwood (in Holt) *Bothenewode* 1323. Probably Old English *bothen* 'rosemary, darnel, or thyme', with *wudu* 'wood'. The word survives in Dorset dialect as *botham*, *bothen* 'corn marigold'.

Bourne Farm (in Piddlehinton) *la Bourne* 1270. 'The stream', from Old

English *burna*.

Bournemouth *la Bournemowthe* 1407. 'The mouth of the stream', from Old English *burna* and *mutha*. The stream is still the Bourne.

Bourton *Bureton* 1212, *Burton* 1244. 'Fortified farmstead', or 'farmstead near a fortified place', from Old English *burh-tūn*.

Boveridge (in Cranborne) *Bovehric* 1086 (Domesday Book), *Bogerugg* 12th century. '(Place) above the ridge', from Old English *bufan* and *hrycg*, or 'bow-shaped, i.e. curved, ridge', from Old English *boga* and *hrycg*.

Bovington (in Wool) *Bovintone* 1086 (Domesday Book), *Bovyngton* 1288. 'Farm called after a man named Bofa', from an Old English personal name with *-ingtūn*.

Bowden (in Kington Magna) *Bouedon* 1332. '(Place) above the hill, i.e. on top of the hill', from Old English *bufan* and *dūn*.

Bowerswain Farm (in Gussage All Saints) *Boresfen* 1288. 'Fen or marsh of a man called Bār', Old English personal name and *fenn*.

Bowldish Pond (in Wimborne St Giles) possibly 'bull pasture', from Old English *bula* and *edisc*, with change by folk etymology if the round pond here was thought to resemble a bowl or a dish.

Bowleaze Cove (near Preston) *Bolheys* 1461, *Bolehaies* 1586. 'Enclosures where bulls were kept', Old English *bula* and *hæg*.

Bowood, North and South (in Netherbury) *Bovewode* 1086 (Domesday Book), *Bouewode* 1288. '(Place) above the wood', from Old English *bufan* and *wudu*.

Bowridge Hill (in Gillingham) *Poghrigge* 1292. Probably 'pouch-shaped ridge', from Old English *pohha* and *hrycg*.

Boys Hill (in Holnest) *Boies hill* 1582. Named from the family of William *de Boys* who was here in the early 14th century.

Boywood Farm (in Mappowder) *Boywode* 1494. Possibly 'wood of a man called Boia', from Old English personal name and *wudu*.

Bradford, '(place at) the broad ford', from Old English *brād* and *ford*: (i) **Bradford Abbas** *Bradan forda* 933 (12th century copy of Saxon charter), *Bradeford* 1086 (Domesday Book), *Braddeford Abbatis* 1386. At a crossing of River Yeo; addition is Latin *abbas* 'abbot', from early possession of this manor by Sherborne Abbey. (ii) **Bradford Farm** (in Pamphill) *Bradeford* 1212, often *Bradeford Brian* from the *Brian de Insula* who gave his name to Bryanston. (iii) **Bradford Peverell** *Bradeford* 1086 (Domesday Book), *Bradeford Peuerel* 1244. At a crossing of River Frome; addition is from *Peverel* family, here in the 13th-14th centuries.

Bradle Farm (in Church Knowle) *Bradelege* 1086 (Domesday Book). 'Broad wood or clearing', from Old English *brād* and *lēah*.

Bradpole *Bratepolle* 1086 (Domesday Book), *Bradepol* 1212. 'Broad pool', from Old English *brād* and *pōl*.

Branksome (in Poole) a recent name, from a house called *Branksome Tower* in the 19th century which in turn was probably named from the setting of Sir Walter Scott's *Lay of the Last Minstrel* published in 1805; Scott's *Branksome Tower* is near Hawick in Roxburghshire, Scotland. *Chine* in Branksome Chine is from Old English *cinu* 'ravine'.

Breach, from Old English *brēc, bræc* 'land broken up for cultivation': (i) **Breach Farm** (in Marnhull) *la Breche* 1482. (ii) **Breach Woods** (in Hilton) *la Brache* 1399.

Bredy Farm (in Burton Bradstock) *Bridie* 1086 (Domesday Book), *Bridie bone uile* 1280. Named from River Bride, see next name. Manorial affix from *de Bonevil* family, here 1285.

Bredy, Little and Long *Bridian* 987 (13th century copy of Saxon charter), *Litelbride, Langebride* 1086 (Domesday Book), *Litlebridie* 1204, *Langebridie* 1244. Both named from River Bride, a Celtic river-name meaning 'gushing or surging stream'. *Long* and *Little* refer to relative shape and size of the two places.

Brenscombe Farm (in Corfe Castle) *Brunescume* 1086 (Domesday Book). 'Valley of a man called Brȳni', Old English personal name and *cumb*.

Briantspuddle (in Affpuddle) *Pidele* 1086 (Domesday Book), *Brianis Pedille* 1465. Named from River Piddle, like Affpuddle itself. Addition *Briants* is from *Brian de Turbervill* who held the manor in the early 14th century (the -*t*- is quite unhistorical). From the 13th century often known as *Pudele Turberville*.

Briar's Wood (in Stockwood) *Priureswode* 1274. 'Wood of the prior (or of a family called Prior)', Middle English *prior* and *wode*. The alteration of *P*- to *B*- first appears in 17th century.

Bride, River see Bredy.

Bridge Lane (in Abbotsbury) *Brugelane* 1492. Self-explanatory.

Bridport *Brideport* 1086 (Domesday Book), *Bridiport* 1157. 'Harbour or market town belonging to or associated with Bredy', from Old English *port* and the name Bredy found in Little and Long Bredy. The name of the river at Bridport, the Brit (earlier the *Woth*), is a 'back-formation' from the place-name.

Brimbley Farm (in Stoke Abbott) *Bromlegam* 12th century. 'Clearing where broom grows', from Old English *brōm* and *lēah*. Brimbley Coombe Farm nearby is *Cumb* 1221, from *cumb* 'valley'.

Brinsham Farm (in Netherbury) *Brinsham* 1288. 'Enclosure of a man called Brȳni', from an Old English personal name and *hamm*.

Brit, River see Bridport.

Broadenham Farm (in Netherbury) *Brodeham* 1268. 'Broad enclosure', from Old English *brād* (dative *brādan*) and *hamm*.

Broadley Wood (in Bryanston) *Bradele* 1334. 'Broad wood or clearing', from Old English *brād* and *lēah*.

Broadmayne *Maine* 1086 (Domesday Book), *Brademaene* 1202, *Brodemaynne* 1288. From Celtic *main* 'a rock, a stone', no doubt with reference to the many large sarsens scattered to the NE of the village (apparently a natural phenomenon, in spite of their resemblance to a man-made stone circle). *Broad-* (Old English *brād)* to distinguish this manor from Little Mayne. Broadmayne was often *Mayne Martel* in medieval times, from the *Martel* family.

Broad Oak (in Symondsbury) *Brode Woke* 1493. 'Large oak-tree', from Old English *brād* and *āc*.

Broadstone (in Poole) first recorded 1765.

Broadwey *Wai(a)* 1086 (Domesday Book), *Bradeweye* 1249. One of several places named from River Wey, an ancient pre-English river-name of unknown origin and meaning. *Broad-* (Old English *brād*) refers to width of the river here or to size of the manor.

Broadwindsor *Windesore* 1086 (Domesday Book), *Windlesor* 1202, *Magna Wyndesor* 1249, *Brodewyndesore* 1324. 'Bank or slope with a windlass', from Old English *windels* and *ōra*. *Broad-* (Latin *magna* 'great') to distinguish this manor from Littlewindsor.

Brockham (in Turnworth) *Brocam* early 13th century. Possibly 'enclosure by a brook', from Old English *brōc* and *hamm,* although there is no brook here now, or from *brocc* 'badger'.

Brockhampton Green (in Buckland Newton) *Brokhampton* 1288. 'Homestead by the brook', from Old English *brōc* and *hām-tūn,* or identical in origin with Brockington Farm.

Brockhill (in Turners Puddle) *Brockholes* 1664. 'Badger holes', from Old English *brocc-hol.*

Brockington Farm (in Gussage All Saints) *Brochemtune* 1086 (Domesday Book). Probably 'farm of the dwellers by the brook', from Old English *brōc, hæme* and *tūn.* It lies beside River Allen.

Bronkham Hill (in Winterborne St Martin) *Bromcomb* 1445. 'Valley where broom grows', from Old English *brōm* and *cumb.*

Broom Hill (in Holt) *Bromehill* in 1591. See next name.

Broomhill Bridge (in Moreton) *Brumel Bridge* 1791, named from Broomhill in Winfrith Newburgh, *Bromhill* 1244, 'broom-covered hill' from Old English *brōm* and *hyll.*

Brownsea Island *Brunkeseye* 1241. Probably 'island of a man called Brūnoc', from an Old English personal name and *ēg*.

Bryanston *Blaneford Brian, Brianeston* 1268. 'Brian's estate', from Old English *tūn*. The man in question was *Brian de Insula* who held this manor (originally *Blaneford* = Blandford) in 13th century.

Buckham (in Beaminster) *Bochenham* 1086 (Domesday Book), *Bukeham* 1244. Probably 'enclosure where male deer or he-goats are kept', from Old English *bucca* and *hamm*.

Buckhorn Weston *Westone* 1086 (Domesday Book), *Boukeresweston* 1275, *Bokerne Weston* 1346. 'West farm or estate', from Old English *west* and *tūn*, perhaps referring to its situation in relation to Gillingham. Manorial affix from Middle English *bouker* 'buck-washer, bleacher' (or the surname derived from it). Possessive *-es* in *Boukeres-* was taken to be plural (thus *-en* as in *oxen*), with later *Bukkehorne* (from 1535) due to folk etymology.

Buckland Newton *Boclond* 854 (14th century copy of Saxon charter), *Bochelande* 1086 (Domesday Book), *Newton Buckland* 1576. From Old English *bōcland* 'charter land', i.e. 'land in which certain rights and privileges were granted by charter'. The relatively recent addition *Newton* is from Sturminster Newton.

Buckland Ripers (near Radipole) *Bocheland* 1086 (Domesday Book), *Boklond Ripers* 1359. Identical in origin with previous name. Manorial addition from the family of *de Riuers* or *de Ripariis* (from Riviere in Normandy) here in 13th century.

Bucknowle House (in Church Knowle) *Bubecnolle* 1285. 'Hill-top of a man called Bubba', from Old English personal name and *cnoll*.

Buckshaw House (in Holwell) *Buggechage* 1194. Probably 'small wood of a woman called Bucge', from Old English *sceaga* and a personal name, or from Middle English *bugge* 'boggart, hobgoblin'.

Bugley (in Gillingham) *Bogeley* 1275. From Old English *lēah* 'wood, clearing', with first element as in previous name.

Bulbarrow Hill (in Stoke Wake) *Buleberwe* 1270. Old English *beorg* 'barrow, tumulus' with *bula* 'bull' or personal name *Bula*.

Bulbury Camp (in Lytchett Minster) *Burlebury, Bulrebury* 1306. Old English *burh* 'earthwork', with reference to the hill-fort here. First part of name is probably 'wood or clearing by the earthwork' from the same word *burh* and Old English *lēah*.

Bullhill (in Alderholt) *Bulhill* 1618, self-explanatory.

Burcombe Farm (in North Poorton) *Burcumbe* 1244. 'Valley with a cottage', from Old English *būr* and *cumb*, or from *burh* 'manor'.

Burleston *Bordelestone* 934 (later copy of Saxon charter), *Burdeleston* 1212. 'Farm or estate of a man called Burdel', from Old English *tūn* and an Old French personal name.

Burngate Farm (in West Lulworth) *Brunnegate* 1262. Probably 'brown gate', from Old English *brūn* and *geat*.

Burning Cliff (in Owermoigne) so called from the spontaneous ignition of the bituminous shale here in 1826.

Burstock *Burewinestoch* 1086 (Domesday Book), *Burgestok* 1200. 'Outlying farm of a woman called Burgwynn or a man called Burgwine', from an Old English personal name and *stoc*.

Burton, 'fortified farmstead' or 'farmstead near a fortification', from Old English *burh-tūn*: (i) **Burton** (in Charminster) *Burton* 1204. Here the *burh* referred to is Poundbury Camp in Dorchester. (ii) **Burton** (in Christchurch) *Buretone* 1100. (iii) **Burton** (in Marnhull) *Burtun* 1244. In medieval times often *(N)ashburton* from nearby Nash Court. (iv) **Burton, East and West** (in Winfrith Newburgh) *Bureton* 1212, *Estburton*, *Westburton* 1280. (v) **Burton, Long** *Burton* 1244, *Langebourton* 1460. 'Long' from the length of the village.

Burton Bradstock *Bridetone* 1086 (Domesday Book), *Briditona* 1244. 'Farm or estate on River Bride', from Old English *tūn*. Late addition *Bradstock* (from 1773) is from Wiltshire abbey of Bradenstoke which held this manor from 13th century.

Burwood (in Cranborne) *Borwode* 1285. Probably 'wood at or near the fortified place', from Old English *burh* and *wudu*.

Bushey (in Corfe Castle) *Burshawe* 1299. Probably 'small wood or copse with a cottage', from Old English *būr* and *sceaga*.

Bussey Stool Farm (in Tarrant Gunville) *Burcyes* 1432, *Burses Stolle* 1590. Named from a family called *Burcy*, here in 14th century. *Stool* is Old English *stōl* 'stool, seat', here 'flat-topped hill'.

Butterwick Wood (in Folke) *Buterwik, Buterwyk* 1288. 'Farm where butter is made', from Old English *butere* and *wīc*.

Buzbury Rings (in Tarrant Keynston) Iron Age enclosure not recorded before 19th century, probably Old English *burh* 'fortified place, earthwork' with an Old English personal name *Beorhtsige*.

Cale, River *Cawel* 10th century, an old Celtic river-name of uncertain origin and meaning.

Cam, River a tributary of Caundle Brook, possibly an old Celtic river-name with a meaning 'crooked, winding'.

Camesworth (in Netherbury) *Kaymmswoth* 1288. An estate on the River *Woth* (now called River Brit) held by a family called *Kaym* or *Caym*, see

Wooth Grange also in this parish.

Canford, Little (in Hampreston) *Parva Caneford* 1263, *Lytel Canefford* 1381. With Latin *parva* 'little', see Canford Magna.

Canford Magna *Cheneford* 1086 (Domesday Book), *Kaneford* 1195, *Greate Canford* 1612. 'Ford of a man called Cana', from an Old English personal name and *ford*. Latin *magna* 'great' to distinguish it from Little Canford across River Stour.

Cann *Canna* early 12th century, *Canne* 1202. Old English *canne* 'can, cup', used topographically for 'a hollow, a deep valley' with reference to the situation of this place in a steeply sided valley.

Canon Hill (in Colehill) perhaps preserving the name of the old Hundred of *Canendone* recorded in Domesday Book, 'Cana's hill', from the Old English personal name found in Canford and *dūn*.

Cards Mill Farm (in Whitchurch Canonicorum) *Cas(i)mulle* 1280. Old English *myln*, first element probably the surname *Case*.

Carey (in Wareham) *Keire* 1220, *Carry* 1318. Perhaps an old Celtic river-name for the lower course of River Piddle or Trent.

Castle Hill (in Cranborne) *Castlehill* 1553, referring to the undated motte and bailey here, first recorded as *Castell* in 1324.

Castleton *Castleton* 1332. 'Farm or estate by the castle', from Old English *tūn*, with reference to Sherborne Castle.

Caswell Farm (in Ryme Intrinseca) *Carsewell* 1332. 'Spring or stream where cress grows', from Old English *cærse* and *wella*.

Catherston Leweston *Chartreston* 1268, *Lesterton* 1316, *Katherston Lewson* 1576. Originally adjacent estates belonging to families called *Charteray* and *Lester*, with Old English *tūn*.

Catsley Farm (in Corscombe) *Catesclive* 1086 (Domesday Book), *Cattescliue* 1244. 'Cliff or steep slope frequented by wild-cats', from Old English *catt* and *clif*. For development, see Rockley.

Cattistock *Cattesstoke* 934, *Stoche* 1086 (Domesday Book), *Cattestok* 1288. 'Secondary settlement of a man called Catt', from Old English *stoc* and a personal name from Old English *catt* 'a cat'.

Caundle, Bishop's and Purse *Candel* 1086 (Domesday Book), *Purscaundel* 1241, *Caundel Bishops* 1294. The meaning of the name Caundle, found in these two names as well as in Caundle Marsh, Caundle Wake and Stourton Caundle, is obscure but may originally have been a name for the chain of hills in the vicinity. *Bishop's* is from the possession of this manor by the Bishop of Salisbury. *Purse* is probably also a manorial addition, the family name of an early owner. Caundle Brook is named from the places.

Caundle Marsh *Candelemers* 1245, *Caundelmersh* 1333. See Bishop's Caundle. From Old English *mersc* 'marsh'.

Caundle Wake (in Bishop's Caundle) *Caundelwak* 1288. See Bishop's Caundle. *Wake* is a manorial addition from the family of that name here in the late 13th century (see also Stoke Wake).

Causeway Farm (near Radipole) *Caucesweie* 1371, *Causweye* 1381. 'Manor on River Wey held by the *Kauz* family', see Broadwey. John *de Kauz* or *le Kauz* held land here in 1299.

Cerne, River an old Celtic river-name identical in origin with River Char, 'stony stream' from Celtic *carn* 'cairn, heap of stones'. It gives name to the three Cernes as well as to Charminster.

Cerne Abbas *Cernel* 987 (13th century copy of Saxon charter), 1086 (Domesday Book), *Cerne* 1175, *Cerne Abbatis* 1288. Like Nether and Up Cerne, named from River Cerne. Latin *abbas* 'abbot' with reference to the abbey here.

Cerne, Nether *Nudernecerna* 1206, *Nethercerne* 1288. *Nether* (from Old English *neotherra*) means 'lower down river'.

Cerne, Up *Obcerne* 1086 (Domesday Book), *Upcerne* 1202. *Up* means 'higher up river' from Old English *upp*.

Chaffeymoor House (in Bourton) *Chauye* 1327. Probably Old English *ceaf* 'chaff' (perhaps here 'rubbish, fallen twigs') and *īeg* 'land partly surrounded by water', with *mōr* 'marshy ground'.

Chalbury (parish) *cheoles burge* 946 (14th century copy of Saxon charter), *Chelesbyr* 1244. 'Fortified place of a man called Cēol', from an Old English personal name and *burh*.

Chalbury (near Preston) *Charlebury* 1452. 'Fort or encampment of the peasants', Old English *ceorl* and *burh*. Chalbury is an Iron Age hill-fort.

Chaldon Herring *Celvedune*, *Calvedone* 1086 (Domesday Book), *Chaluedon Hareng* 1243. 'Hill where calves are pastured', from Old English *cealf* and *dūn*. Manorial addition from the *Harang* family, here from the 12th century, see Herrison, Langton Herring and Winterborne Herringston.

Chaldon, West, or Chaldon Boys (in Chaldon Herring) *West Chalvedon* 1269, *Chalvedon Boys* 1280. 'West' in relation to Chaldon Herring, *Boys* from the family of *de Bosco* or *Boys*, here from the 13th century.

Challow Farm (in Corfe Castle) *Challway* 1716. Probably 'chalk way', from Old English *cealc* and *weg*.

Chalmington (in Cattistock) *Chelmyntone* 934 (later copy of Saxon charter), *Chelminton* 1212. 'Farm called after a man named Cēolhelm or Cēolmund', Old English personal name and *-ingtūn*.

Chamberlayne's Farm (in Bere Regis) *Chaumberleynesmylle* 1411. Named from the *Chamberlayn* family, in the area from 13th century.

Champernhayes Farm (in Wootton Fitzpaine) *Chapronheys* 1440. 'Enclosures of the Champernon family', Old English *hæg*.

Chantmarle (in Cattistock) *Chauntemerle* 1288. Named from the *Chauntemerle* family, recorded with lands here from 13th century.

Chapel Court (in Mosterton) *Chapell* (manor of) 1486.

Chapel Marsh (in Beaminster) *Chappell Marsh* 1615. Named from a chapel here recorded in the 13th century.

Chapman's Pool (in Worth Matravers) *schort mannes pol* 948 (15th century copy of Saxon charter), *Shortmanpole* 1489. 'Small pool used in common', from Old English *sceort, mænnes* and *pōl*, or 'pool of a man called Sceortmann' from an Old English personal name. Modern spelling first recorded in 1811.

Char, River Celtic river-name with same origin as River Cerne.

Charborough House (in Morden) *Cerebrie* 1086 (Domesday Book), *Chereberge* 1212. Old English *beorg* 'a hill, a barrow' with either an old Celtic name for River Winterborne (on which Charborough is situated) identical with River Cerne, or Old English *cearr* 'bend' (with reference to gentle curve in river here).

Charing Cross (in Alderholt) at a cross-roads, no doubt named from the well-known London place (OE *cerring* 'a bend').

Charlestown (in Chickerell) first recorded 1893.

Charlton, 'farm or estate belonging to the peasants', from Old English *ceorl* and *tūn*: (i) **Charlton Dairy Farm** (in Woodlands) *Cherleton* 1266. (ii) **Charlton Higher Down** (in Charminster) *Cherlton* 1226. (iii) **Charlton Marshall** *Cerletone* 1086 (Domesday Book), *Cherleton Marescal* 1288. Addition from *Marshall* family, here in 13th century, see Sturminster Marshall.

Charminster (parish) *Cerminstre* 1086 (Domesday Book), *Cerneministr* 1223. 'Church on River Cerne', from Old English *mynster*. See under Cerne for the meaning of the river-name.

Charminster (in Bournemouth) recent name for a modern district of the town, presumably transferred from the previous place.

Charmouth *Cearn* 737 (12th century copy of Saxon charter), *Cernemude* 1086 (Domesday Book), *Cernemuth* 13th century. Named from River Char (*Cearn*), with Old English *mūtha* 'mouth'.

Chartknolle (in Stoke Abbott) *Charteray* 1240. Probably a manorial name from a family so called, see Catherston Leweston, with later addition of *knoll* 'a hillock'.

Chebbard Farm (in Dewlish) *Scaborthe* 1335, probably to be associated with *Ceatwanberge* 870, thus possibly 'hill or border of a man called Ceatwa', from an Old English personal name and *beorg* or *bord.*

Chedington *Chedinton* 1194. 'Farm called after a man named Cedd or Cedda', from an Old English personal name and *-ingtūn.*

Chelborough, East and West *Celberge* 1086 (Domesday Book), *Estchelberewe* 1343, *Westchelbergh* 1346. Possibly 'hill of a man called Cēola', from an Old English personal name and *beorg*, but the first element could alternatively be Old English *ceole* 'throat, gorge' or *cealc* 'chalk' (referring to chalk cap of Castle Hill).

Chescombe Farm (in Winterborne Whitechurch) *Churchecombe* 1539. 'Church valley', from Old English *cirice* and *cumb,* with reference to St Mary's Church in Winterborne Whitechurch.

Cheselbourne *Chiselburne* 870 (15th century copy of Saxon charter), *Ceseburne* 1086 (Domesday Book), *Cheselburne* 1212. 'Gravel stream', from Old English *cisel* and *burna.*

Chesil Beach *the Chisil, Chisille bank* 1535-43. From Old English *cisel* 'shingle'. This ridge of pebbles extends along the coast for some 16 miles, and gives its name to the village of Chesil (recorded as *Chesill* 1608) on the Isle of Portland.

Chetnole *Chetenoll* 1242, *Chattecnolle* 1268. 'Hill-top or hillock of a man called Ceatta', from Old English personal name and *cnoll.*

Chetterwood (in Moor Crichel) *Chetred* 1215. Possibly from Celtic *cēd* 'wood' with Celtic *rid* 'ford' or Old English *rīth* 'stream'; there is now no ford or stream, but there is a marked valley.

Chettle *Ceotel* 1086 (Domesday Book), *Chetel* 12th century. Probably Old English *ceotol* 'kettle', here in topographical sense 'deep valley surrounded by hills', referring to situation of village.

Chettle Head Copse (in Pentridge) *cheotoles heafde* 955 (14th century copy of Saxon charter), *Chetelesheved* 1281. Old English *ceotol* 'kettle' used in topographical sense as in previous name, with *hēafod* 'head', here 'hill, ridge' or 'upper end of valley'.

Chewton Bunny (in Christchurch) *Chiventon* 12th century, *Chyveton* 1280. Probably 'estate of a man called Cifa', from an Old English personal name and *tūn*. Bunny (*la Bonye* 14th century, possibly 'marshy land with reeds' from Old English *bune* and *īeg*) refers to the chine here.

Chickerell *Cicherelle* 1086 (Domesday Book), *Chikerel* 1227. This unique name remains obscure. It is one of the few Dorset names that have not yet been satisfactorily explained.

Chideock *Cidihoc* 1086 (Domesday Book), *Cidioc* 1240. 'Wooded place', from a derivative of Celtic *cēd* 'wood'. The river-name Chid is a back-formation from the place-name.

Chilbridge Farm (in Pamphill) *Chelebruga* 12th century. Old English *brycg*, probably here 'causeway through marshy ground', with Old English *ceole* 'channel, gorge' or personal name *Cēola*.

Chilcombe *Ciltecome* 1086 (Domesday Book), *Chiltecumb* 1268. Probably 'valley at a hill-slope called *Cilte*', from an Old English or pre-English hill-name and Old English *cumb*.

Childhay (in Broadwindsor) *Childheya* 1234, *Childehey* 1244. 'Enclosure of the young noblemen', from Old English *cild* and *hæg*.

Child Okeford see under Okeford.

Chilfrome *Frome* 1086 (Domesday Book), *Childefrome* 1206. 'Estate on River Frome belonging to the young noblemen', from Old English *cild*. In Domesday Book the manor is stated to have formerly belonged jointly to three thanes or noblemen.

Chilmore (in Hilton) *Childemore* 1399. 'Moor or marshy ground of the young noblemen', from Old English *cild* and *mōr*.

Christchurch *Tweoxneam* 10th century (Anglo-Saxon Chronicle), *Twynham* 934 (later copy of Saxon charter), *Thuinam* 1086 (Domesday Book), *Cristeschirche of Twynham* 1318. The old name means '(place) betwixt or between the streams', from Old English *betweoxn* or *betwēonan* and *ēa* (dative plural *ēam*), referring to its situation between Rivers Stour and Avon. The newer name is self-explanatory.

Christmas Close (in Wareham) first recorded in 1707 and named from the family of one Robert *Crissmasse* mentioned in 1532.

Church Knowle *Cnolle, Chenolle* 1086 (Domesday Book), *Churchecnolle* 1346. Originally 'the hill-top', from Old English *cnoll*, later with the addition of Old English *cirice* 'church'. There is mention of a priest here at the time of Domesday book.

Clandon (Hill) (in Winterborne St Martin) *Clandon* 1594. 'Clean (i.e. cleared) hill', from Old English *clæne* and *dūn*.

Clapgate (in Colehill) first recorded 1811. 'Gate that shuts to on its own', probably a gate to Holt forest.

Clatcombe Farm (near Sherborne) *Klatcombe* 1569. 'Valley where burdock grows', from Old English *clāte* and *cumb*.

Claylake (in Verwood) thus in 1846, Old English *lacu* 'stream'.

Claywell (in Studland) *Cleywoll* 1332. 'Clay spring or stream', from Old English *clæg* and *wella*.

Clift, The (in Shillingstone) *La Clive* 1270. From Old English *clif* 'cliff, bank'; it is beside River Stour.

Clifton Maybank *Cliftune* 1012, *Clistone* 1086 (Domesday Book), *Clifton*

Mabank 1319. 'Farm or estate on the hill slope or river bank', from Old English *clif* and *tūn*. Manorial addition from the family of William *Malbeenc* (here in Domesday Book).

Clinger Farm (in Buckland Newton) *Clehangre* 1206. 'Clayey wooded slope', from Old English *clæg* and *hangra*.

Clyffe Farm and House (in Tincleton) *Clyue* 934 (later copy of Saxon charter), *Clive* 1086 (Domesday Book). '(Place) at the cliff or hill-slope', from Old English *clif*.

Cobb (in Lyme Regis) *la Cobbe* 1295. Referring to the famous semi-circular pier, from Old English *cobb* 'a rounded mass'.

Cobley Farm (in Pentridge) *Cobl(e)y* 17th century. Old English *lēah* 'wood, clearing', possibly with Old English *cobb* 'rounded mass' (perhaps here 'hill') or an Old English personal name *Cobba*.

Cockhill Farm (in Stourton Caundle) *Cokhull* 1332. 'Hill frequented by woodcocks or other wild birds', from Old English *cocc* and *hyll*, or from *cocc* meaning 'heap, hillock' .

Cocknowle (in Church Knowle) *Kokenulle, Kokenhule* 14th century. Possibly 'hill, or hollow, frequented by woodcocks', from Old English *cocc* and *hyll* or *hylu*.

Coker's Frome (in Stinsford) recorded thus from 18th century, called *East Froome* in 17th century. 'Manor on River Frome of the Coker family', this family being noted here from 1433.

Cold Harbour (in Wareham) thus in 18th century, 'cold or cheerless shelter', from Old English *cald* and *here-beorg*.

Colehill *Colhulle* 1431, *Collehill* 1547. Old English *hyll* 'hill' with either Old English *col* 'charcoal' or *coll* 'hill'.

Cole Hill Wood (in Winterborne Came) *Cold(e)hull* 1406. 'Cold hill', from Old English *cald* and *hyll*.

Cole Street Farm (in East Stour) *Colstrete* 1504. Probably 'street along which charcoal was carried', from Old English *col* and *stræt*.

Cole Wood (in Wool) *Colewode* 1452. Probably 'wood where charcoal was burnt', from Old English *col* and *wudu*.

Colmer Farm (in Marshwood) *Colemer* 1332. 'Cool pool', from Old English *col* and *mere*.

Coltleigh Farm (in Mapperton) *Cottelegh* 1244. 'Wood or clearing of a man called Cotta', from Old English personal name and *lēah*.

Colway (in Lyme Regis) *Coleweye* 1243, *Colweheye* 1268. Probably 'enclosure by charcoal way', from Old English *col* and *weg* with the addition of *hæg*.

Combe Almer (in Sturminster Marshall) *Cumbe* 1228, *Combe Almere*

1327. 'The valley (near Almer)', from Old English *cumb.*

Combs Ditch (near Winterborne Whitechurch) *Cunucces dich* 942 (15th century copy of Saxon charter), from a Celtic word *conōg* of doubtful meaning, with Old English *dīc* 'ditch'. This earthwork is a boundary bank and ditch of Iron Age origin, which also gave its name to a Hundred.

Compton, 'farm or estate in a valley', from Old English *cumb* and *tūn*: (i) **Compton Abbas** *Cumtune* 956 (14th century copy of Saxon charter), *Cuntone* 1086 (Domesday Book), *Cumpton Abbatisse* 1293. This manor belonged to Shaftesbury Abbey from 956, hence the addition *Abbas,* a reduced form of Latin *abbatissa* 'abbess'. (ii) **Compton, Over and Nether** *Cumtun* 951 (12th century copy of Saxon charter), *Contone* 1086 (Domesday Book), *Ouerecumton* 1268, *Nethercumpton* 1288. Additions *Over* and *Nether* mean 'higher' and 'lower' respectively. (iii) **Compton Valence** *Contone* 1086 (Domesday Book), *Compton Valance* 1280. Manorial addition from William *de Valencia*, Earl of Pembroke, who was granted the manor in 1252. (iv) **Compton, West, or Compton Abbas West** *Comptone* 934 (later copy of Saxon charter), *Contone* 1086 (Domesday Book), *Cumpton Abbatis* 1291, *West Compton* 1811. Addition is Latin *abbas* 'abbot' because this manor belonged to Milton Abbey. Now usually called West Compton to distinguish it from the other Compton Abbas.

Conegar Hill (in Broadwindsor) named from *Le Conyngere* 1496, from Middle English *coninger* 'a rabbit warren'.

Conygar Hill (in Winterborne Herringston) first recorded in the 19th century, identical in origin with the previous name.

Coombe, '(place in) the valley', from Old English *cumb*: (i) **Coombe (Down Hill)** (in Beaminster) *Combe* 1327, *Coomdowne* 1625. (ii) **Coombe** (in Bradford Abbas) *Comb* 1332. (iii) **Coombe Bottom** (in Corfe Castle) *cumb* 948 (15th century copy of Saxon charter), *la Combe* 14th century. (iv) **Coombe Farm** (in Castleton) *Combe* 1316. (v) **Coombe, Higher and Lower** (in Litton Cheney) *Cumbe* 1220. (vi) **Coombe Keynes** *Cume* 1086 (Domesday Book), *Combe Kaynes* 1299. *Keynes* is a manorial addition from the family of William *de Cahaignes,* who held the manor in 1199.

Coppleridge (in Motcombe) *Copidockridge* 1609. 'Ridge at the pollarded oak-tree', from Old English *coppod, āc* and *hrycg*.

Corfe Castle *Corf* 955 (14th century copy of Saxon charter), *Corffe Castell* 1302. 'A cutting, a pass', from Old English *corf,* aptly describing the gap in the central ridge of the Purbeck Hills at this place. In the Anglo-Saxon Chronicle during the 11th-12th centuries it was sometimes called *Corfesgeate*, 'gap (Old English *geat*) called *Corf*'. The castle here is mentioned in Domesday Book, but *Castle* is not attached to village name until 14th century.

Corfe Hill (near Radipole) *Corfhull* 1303. 'Hill at a cutting or gap', from Old English *corf* and *hyll*.

Corfe Mullen *Corf* 1086 (Domesday Book), *Corf le Mulin* 1176. From Old English *corf* 'a cutting or pass', with reference to its situation between two hills. Addition *Mullen* is from Old French *molin* 'a mill', referring to the valuable mill here which rendered 20 shillings (a high value) at the time of Domesday Book.

Corner, The (in Motcombe) the home of John *atte Cornere* 1381, that is John 'at the corner or nook', from Middle English *corner*.

Corscombe *Corigescumb* 1014 (12th century copy of Saxon charter), *Cor(ie)scumbe* 1086 (Domesday Book), *Corescumb* 1244. 'Valley of a stream called Cori', from Old English *cumb* and the old (pre-English) name of the stream rising south of the village.

Corton (in Portesham) *Corfetone* 1086 (Domesday Book), *Corfton* 1204. 'Farm by a cutting or gap', from Old English *corf* and *tūn*.

Coryates (in Portesham) *Corf getes* 1024 (Saxon charter), *le Corueyatis* 1473. 'Gate at the cutting or gap', from Old English *corf* and *geat*. The final *-s* is genitive, cf. the earliest spelling: *Corf getes westran cotan*, 'the more westerly cottages of *Corf gete*'.

Cothayes Dairy (in Hilton) *Cotehay* 1412. 'Enclosure by a cottage', from Old English *cot* and *hæg*.

Cowdon Hill (in Charminster) *Cowdon* 14th century. 'Cow down or hill', from Old English *cū* and *dūn*.

Cowgrove (in Pamphill) *Cugrave* 1288. 'Cow grove or copse', from Old English *cū* and *grāf*.

Cowherd Shute Farm (in Motcombe) *Cowards Shoot* 1811. From the surname *Coward* with *shute* 'steep slope'.

Crab Farm (in Shapwick) not on early record, but presumably an allusion to the legend of the 'Shapwick monster' (in local proverb a term for any unusual object, since an ordinary crab was considered a monster by the wise man of Shapwick).

Crab Orchard (in Verwood) Old English *crabbe* 'crab-apple'.

Cranborne *Creneburne* 1086 (Domesday Book), *Craneburna* 1163. 'Stream frequented by cranes or herons', from Old English *cran* and *burna*, originally with reference to the stream here now called River Crane (a back-formation from the place-name).

Cranborne Chase first recorded in 1236, from Middle English *chace* 'tract of land for hunting wild animals'.

Crate Wood (in Woolland) *Croftewood* 1384. 'Wood by the small enclosure', from Old English *croft* and *wudu*.

Crawford Bridge (in Spettisbury) 'the bridge of *Crauford*' 1242, *Craufordesbrigge* 1337. 'Ford frequented by crows', from Old English *crāwe* and *ford*, with *brycg*. The ford gave its name to the former manor of *Great Crawford* in Spetisbury (*Craveford* 1086) and to Tarrant Crawford on the other side of River Stour.

Creech Barrow (in Church Knowle) giving name to East Creech in this parish and to Creech Grange and West Creech in Steeple. The name is *Cric, Criz, Crist* 1086 (Domesday Book), *Crich* 1224, *Weste Crych* 1324, *Estcriche* 1337. This is the oldest name in Purbeck, from Celtic *crūg* 'mound, hill', originally with reference to Creech Barrow itself, a conspicuous conical hill and an important early landmark.

Creech Hill Farm (in Wimborne St Giles) recorded late, but perhaps identical in origin with Crichel; the hill is 300 feet high and stands where the boundaries of three parishes meet.

Crendell (in Alderholt) *Crendall* 1620. From Old English *crundel* 'a pit, a quarry' (with reference to a clay or chalk pit).

Crichel, Long *Circel* 1086 (Domesday Book), *Langecrechel* 1208. A very old name, from Celtic *crūg* 'mound, hill' to which an explanatory Old English *hyll* 'hill' was added at an early date. The hill referred to is now called Crichel Down (from Old English *dūn* 'hill, down'). *Long* distinguishes this place from Moor Crichel.

Crichel, Moor *Mor Kerchel* 1212. For the origin of Crichel, see previous name. *Moor* is from Old English *mōr* 'marshy ground'.

Cripplestyle (in Alderholt) probably 'stile that could be crept through (by sheep)', from Old English *crypel* and *stigel*.

Cripton (in Winterborne Came) *Cribbeton* 1457. 'Farm with a crib, cattle farm', from Old English *cribb* and *tūn*.

Crocker's Knap (in Leigh) probably to be associated with *Crockeresrewe* 13th century, from Old English *croccere* 'a potter', *ræw* 'row of houses or trees', *cnæpp* 'hill-top, hillock'.

Crockerton Hill (in Cranborne) probably to be associated with *Crokkerneweye* 1325, 'way to the pottery', Old English *crocc-ærn*.

Crook Hill (in Corscombe) *Cruc* 841 (12th century copy of Saxon charter), *Crokehulle* 1407. An ancient name, from Celtic *crūg* 'hill' to which an explanatory Old English *hyll* 'hill' has been added.

Cruxton (in Maiden Newton) *Frome* 1086 (Domesday Book), *Fromma Johannis Croc* 1178, *Crocston* 1195. 'Estate on River Frome (of John Croc)', later 'Croc's farm', from Old English *tūn*.

Cudnell (in Kinson) *Codnell* 1520. Possibly 'hill or nook of a man called Cuda', from an Old English personal name and *hyll* or *healh*.

Culeaze House (in Bere Regis) *Culyes* 1617. 'Cow pasture', from Old English *cū* and *læs*.

Cut Mill (in Hinton St Mary) *Cuttemylle, Cutmyll* 16th century. 'Mill with a water-channel', from Middle English *cut* and *myln*.

Daggons (in Alderholt) *Daggans* 1553. Named from the family of Richard *Dagon,* here in the 14th century.

Dancing Ledge (in Langton Matravers) thus in 1811, perhaps so called from the action of waves breaking over the flat rock ledges.

Darknoll Farm (in Okeford Fitzpaine) *Derkenhull* 1286. 'The dark hill', from Old English *deorc* (dative *-an*) and *hyll*. It gives name to Darknoll Brook.

Deadmoor Common (in Fifehead Neville) *Deadmore* 1736, probably *dead* in the sense 'disused' with *mōr* 'marshy ground' .

Dean, 'the valley', from Old English *denu*: (i) **Dean** (in Sixpenny Handley) *la Dene* 1280. (ii) **Dean Farm, Deans Leaze Farm** (in Witchampton) *La Dene* 1243, *Deane's Leaze* 1633, with *læs* 'pasture'. (iii) **Dean Hill** (in Studland) *Dene* 1449.

Deanland (in Sixpenny Handley) *Daine Lane* 1664. 'Lane in a valley', from Old English *denu* and *lane.*

Decoy Heath (in Wareham) first recorded in 1811, from *decoy* 'pool with netted approaches for the capture of wildfowl'.

Densham Farm (in Folke) *Denesham* 1332. Possibly 'enclosure of a man called Dene', from an Old English personal name and *hamm*.

Deverel Farm (in Milborne St Andrew) *Muleborn* 1261, *Muleburn Deverell* 1316. Originally a manor on the same 'mill stream' as Milborne St Andrew itself, held by the family of *Deverell* (from Deverill in Wiltshire) from the mid-13th century.

Devil's Brook see Dewlish.

Dewlands Common (in Verwood) ground where dew fell heavily.

Dewlish *Devenis* 1086 (Domesday Book), *Deueliz* 1194. Originally the name of the stream here, a Celtic name meaning 'dark stream'. The modern name of the stream, Devil's Brook, is an interesting example of folk etymology: the name must at one time have been associated with the word 'devilish'.

Dibberford (in Broadwindsor) *Dibberwurthe* 1001-12 (Saxon writ), *Diberwurth* 1244. 'Enclosure of a man called Dycgbeorht', from an Old English personal name and *worth*. The substitution of *ford* for the final element dates from the 16th century.

Didlington Farm (in Chalbury) *Didelingtune* 946 (14th century copy of Saxon charter), *Dedilintone* 1086 (Domesday Book). 'Farm called after a man named Dydel', from an Old English personal name and -*ingtūn*.

Divelish, River an old Celtic river-name, same origin as Dewlish.

Dodding's Farm (in Bere Regis) *Bere* 1086 (Domesday Book), *la Doddingg* 1268. 'Part of Bere at or called Dodding', this name meaning either 'place characterized by a rounded hill-top' from *dodde* and -*ing*, or 'place of a man called Dodda' from an Old English personal name.

Dogbury (in Minterne Magna) *Doggeneberwe* 941 (14th century copy of Saxon charter), *Doggebery* 1270. 'Dogs' hill, hill frequented by dogs', from Old English *dogga* and *beorg*.

Donedge Lodge Farm (in Motcombe) *Donnedge-lodge* 1627. Probably 'edge or end of the down', from Old English *dūn* and *ecg*.

Dorchester *Durnovaria* 4th century (Antonine Itinerary), *Dornwaraceaster* 864 (12th century copy of Saxon charter), *Dorecestre* 1086 (Domesday Book). The original name of this Roman city, *Durnovaria*, is Celtic, perhaps meaning 'place with fist-sized pebbles'. The Anglo-Saxons added Old English *ceaster* 'city' to a reduced form of this name.

Dorset *Dorset* 891 (14th century copy of Saxon charter), *Dornsaetum* late 9th century (Anglo-Saxon Chronicle), *Dorsete* 1086 (Domesday Book). Originally a tribal name, 'the people of the region about Dorchester', from *Dorn-* (a reduced form of *Dornwaraceaster* = Dorchester) and Old English *sæte* 'dwellers'.

Dottery (in Allington) *Dawtry Close* 1557, perhaps from a surname.

Dowerfield Farm (in Long Bredy) *Dowerland* 1431, *Dowrefielde* 1611. 'Land or field given as a dowry', Middle English *dowere*.

Downshay Farm (in Worth Matravers) *Dunshay* 1586. Probably 'Dun's enclosure', from the surname *Dun(n)* and Old English *hæg*.

Drimpton (in Broadwindsor) *Dremeton* 1244. 'Farm or estate of a man called Dreama', from an Old English personal name and *tūn*.

Droop (in Hazelbury Bryan) *Thorpe* 1580, *Throop, Thrupp* 1607. From Old English *throp* 'an outlying farm, a secondary settlement'.

Druce Farm (in Puddletown) *Drewes* 1431. 'Estate belonging to Drew', the man in question being the 13th century *Drew Bardolf* whose family gave name to the nearby Bardolf Manor.

Duddle Farm and Heath (in Puddletown) *Doddle* 1270, *Duddell* 1459. Perhaps 'small rounded hill-top', from a derivative of the word *dodde* possibly present in Dodding's Farm in Bere Regis.

Dudmoor Farm (in Christchurch) *Duddemore* 1269. 'Marshy land of a man called Dudda', from Old English personal name and *mōr*.

Dudsbury, Duds Bury Camp (in West Parley) *Dodesberie* 1086 (Domesday Book), *Dudesbir* 1236. 'Fortified place associated with a man called Dudd', from an Old English personal name and *burh*, with reference to the Iron Age hill-fort here.

Dullar Farm (in Lytchett Matravers) *Dulre* 1268. A difficult name, but possibly 'house in a valley', Old English *dulu* and *ærn*.

Dunbury (in Winterborne Houghton) *Dunbaro* 1603. 'Barrow on the down', from Old English *dūn* and *beorg*.

Duncliffe Hill (in Stour Provost) *Dunclive* 1247. 'Dark escarpment', from Old English *dunn* and *clif*.

Dungrove Hill (in Tarrant Gunville) *Dongroue* 1408. 'Copse on the down or hill', from Old English *dūn* and *grāf*.

Dunster Farm, Little (in Marshwood) *Dunestrewe* 1220. 'Dun's tree', from Old English *trēow* and a personal name or surname.

Duntish (in Buckland Newton) *dounen tit* 941 (14th century copy of Saxon charter), *Donetys* 1268. 'Pasture on a hill', Old English *dūn* and *etisc*.

Durdle Door (in West Lulworth) *Dirdale Door* 1811. Probably from Old English *thyrelod* 'pierced' with *duru* 'door, opening'.

Durlston Bay and Head (in Swanage) thus in 1774, probably 'rock with a hole in it' from Old English *thyrel* and *stān*, perhaps referring to some coastal feature that has now disappeared.

Durweston *Derwinestone* 1086 (Domesday Book), *Durwinestona* 1166. 'Farm or estate of a man called Dēorwine', from an Old English personal name and *tūn*.

Earl's Hill (in Tarrant Gunville) *Earles hill* 1618. The manor of Tarrant Gunville was held in turn by the earls of Gloucester and Hertford, of March, and of Cambridge.

East Brook (in Wimborne Minster) *Byestebrouk* 1286. '(Place) to the east of the brook', from Old English *bī*, *ēastan* and *brōc*, with reference to its situation by River Allen.

Eastbury House (in Tarrant Gunville) *Estbury* 1391. From Middle English *bury* 'manor house', see Westbury Farm in same parish.

Easthay Farm (in Thorncombe) *Estehegh* 1356. 'East enclosure', from Old English *ēast* and *hæg*.

Eastcombe Wood (in Shillingstone) from *cumb* 'valley'.

Eastington Farm (in Worth Matravers) *Estinton* 1209. '(Land) east in the village', from Old English *ēast*, *in* and *tūn*.

East Moors Farm (in St Leonards and St Ives) *Great or East Moors* 1591, named in relation to West Moors.

Easton (on Isle of Portland) *Eston* 1323. 'East farm or village', from Old English *ēast* and *tūn,* in contrast with Weston.

Ebblake (in Verwood) *Abbelake* 1280. Probably 'stream of a man called Abba', from an Old English personal name and *lacu,* originally with reference to Ebblake Stream.

Eccliffe (in Gillingham) *Eggcliue* 1292. Probably 'bank of a man called Ecga', Old English personal name and *clif.* The place is on River Stour.

Edmondsham *Amedesham* 1086 (Domesday Book), *Edmundesham* 1195. 'Homestead or enclosure of a man called Ēadmōd or Ēadmund', from an Old English personal name and *hām* or *hamm.*

Eggardon Farms and Hill (in Askerswell) *Giochresdone* 1086, *Jekeresdon* 1204. 'Hill or down of a man called Eohhere', from an Old English personal name and *dūn.*

Egliston (in Tyneham) *Egelineston* 1202, *Eglyneston* 1288. 'Farm or estate of a man called Eggelin', from Old English *tūn* and a Continental Germanic personal name.

Ellston Hill (in Sydling St Nicholas) *Helistun* 1227, *Eliston* 1293. Possibly 'estate of a man called Eli', from Old English *tūn* and a personal name.

Elwell (in Upwey) *Helewill* 1212, *Hellewell* 1249. 'The healthy spring', or 'the spring which heals', or 'the spring of good fortune', from either Old English *hæle* 'healthy', *hælu* 'health', or *hæl* 'good fortune', with *wella.* The reference may well be to the spring called Wishing Well where River Wey rises about half a mile from here.

Elwell Farms and Lodge (in Netherbury) *Ellewell* 1332. Possibly 'spring or stream of a man called Ella', from an Old English personal name and *wella,* or from Old English *ellen* 'an elder-tree'.

Elworth (in Abbotsbury) *Aleurde* 1086 (Domesday Book), *Elleworthe* 1221. 'Enclosure of a man called Ella', from an Old English personal name and *worth.*

Empool Bottom and Heath (in West Knighton) from late 18th century, possibly 'even or smooth pool' from Old English *emn* and *pōl,* with *botm* 'valley bottom'.

Encombe (in Corfe Castle) *Hennecumbe* 1244. 'Valley of the hens (i.e. water-hens or other wild birds)', Old English *henn* and *cumb.*

Enmore Green (in Shaftesbury) *Hendemer* 1258, *Enedemere* 1275. 'Duck pool', from Old English *ened* and *mere,* with later addition of Green.

Ensbury (in Kinson) *Eynesburgh* 1463. Probably 'fortified place associated with a man called Ægen', from an Old English personal name and *burh.*

Evershot *Teversict* 1201, *Evershet* 1286. Probably 'corner or nook of land frequented by wild boar', from Old English *eofor* and *scēat* or *scīete*. Initial *T-* in the first form may be from the preposition *at*.

Eye Mead (in Pamphill) *Eye* 1253, *Ymede* 1468. From Old English *īeg* 'island', with *mǣd* 'meadow'. It is encircled by River Stour and its tributaries.

Eype (in Symondsbury) *Est yep* 1300, *Yepe* 1365. From Old English *gēap* 'a steep place', with *ēast* 'east' in the earliest form.

Farnham *Fern(e)ham* 1086 (Domesday Book), *Farnham* 1199. 'Homestead or enclosure where ferns grow', Old English *fearn* and *hām* or *hamm*.

Farrington (in Iwerne Courtney) *Ferendone* 1285, *Farendon* 1315. 'Fern-covered hill', from Old English *fearn* and *dūn*.

Feltham Farm (in Silton) *Fyletham* 1327. 'Hay enclosure', from Old English *filethe* and *hamm*.

Fernbrook Farm (in Motcombe) *Fernbroc* 1251. Self-explanatory, from Old English *fearn* and *brōc*, with reference to the stream still called Fern Brook, a tributary of River Lodden.

Ferndown (in Hampreston) *Fyrne* 1321, from either Old English *fergen* 'wooded hill' or *fierne* 'ferny place', with later addition of *down*.

Fiddleford (in Okeford Fitzpaine) *Fitelford* 1244. 'Ford of a man called Fitela', from an Old English personal name and *ford*.

Field Grove (in Durweston) *Fylgrove* 1564, *Feyldegrove Woodd* 1567. 'Grove in open country', from Old English *feld* and *grāf*.

Fifehead Magdalen *Fifhide* 1086 (Domesday Book), *Fifyde Maudaleyne* 1388. '(Estate of) five hides', from Old English *fīf* and *hīd*. The manor was assessed at five hides in Domesday Book, a hide being originally the area of land that would support one free family and its dependants. *Magdalen* from dedication of church.

Fifehead Neville *Fifhide* 1086 (Domesday Book), *Fyfhud Neuyle* 1287. Identical in origin with previous name. Manorial affix from the family of William *de Nevill* who was here in the mid-13th century; the family came from Neville or Neuville in France.

Fifehead St Quintin (in Fifehead Neville) *Fifhide* 1086 (Domesday Book), *Fifhide Quintyn* 1268. Identical in origin with Fifehead Neville. Manorial affix from the family of *de Sancto Quintino*, here in the 13th century, see Frome St Quintin.

Filcombe Farm (in Chideock) *Vilcumbe* 13th century. 'Valley where hay is made', from Old English *filethe* and *cumb*.

Filford (in Netherbury) *Filleforde* 1327. Probably 'ford by the clearing where hay is made', Old English *filethe*, *lēah* and *ford*.

Fitzworth Farm (in Corfe Castle) *Fitoure* 1545. Probably 'shore subject to dispute', from Old English *fitt* and *ōra,* with replacement of second element by Old English *worth* 'enclosure'.

Fleet *Flete, Flote* 1086 (Domesday Book), *Fleota* 1213. From Old English *flēot* 'estuary, inlet', referring to the stretch of water called East and West Fleet between Chesil Beach and the mainland.

Flower's Barrow (in East Lulworth) *Flouresberi* 1381, *Flouresbury* 1462. From Old English *burh* 'pre-English earthwork' with reference to the hill-fort here. The first element could be Old English *flōr* 'a floor' or the surname of some medieval owner.

Folke *Folk* 1244, *Folke* 1337. 'The folk or people', from Old English *folc,* indicating 'land held (in common) by the people'.

Font le Roi (in Folke) *Fontleroy Mershe* 1582. Named from the *Fauntleroy* family, here from the 13th century.

Fontmell Magna *Funtemel* 877 (15th century copy of Saxon charter), *Fontemale* 1086 (Domesday Book), *Magnam Funtemell* 1391. Originally the name of Fontmell Brook, 'stream or spring by the bare hill' from Celtic *funtōn* and *mailo-.* Latin *magna* is 'great'.

Fontmell Parva (in Child Okeford) *Parva Funtemel* 1360. With Latin *parva* 'little' to distinguish it from Fontmell Magna.

Ford Farms (in Netherbury) *la Forde* 1288, Old English *ford.*

Forde Abbey (in Thorncombe) *Ford* 1189, *Forda* 1204. '(Place by) the ford' (over River Axe), from Old English *ford.* The Cistercian abbey was founded in 1141.

Fordington (in Dorchester) *Fortitone* 1086 (Domesday Book), *Fordin(g)ton* 1155. Probably 'farm at the ford place', from Old English *ford, -ing* and *tūn.* The ford was no doubt on River Frome.

Forest Farm and Forest Side (in Gillingham) named from the royal forest of Gillingham which is recorded in 13th century.

Forston (in Charminster) *Fosardeston* 1236. 'Manor or estate of the Forsard family', from Old English *tūn.* This family was here from the early 13th century. Forston is probably *Cerne(l)* in Domesday Book (from its situation on River Cerne).

Fortuneswell (on Isle of Portland) first recorded 1608, 'lucky well or spring', or 'well or spring in which fortunes could be told'.

Fossil, East and West (in Winfrith Newburgh and Chaldon Herring respectively) *Foresteshull* 1227, *West foreshull* 1319, *Estforshull* 1398. Old English *hyll* 'hill', first element probably Old English *forst* 'ridge', or an Old English personal name *Forst.*

Frampton *Frantone* 1086 (Domesday Book), *Fromton* 1188. 'Farm or estate on River Frome', from Old English *tūn.*

France Farm (in Stourpaine) *Franc'* 1368, earlier called *Nodford* 1086 (Domesday Book), *Notfordlocky* 1265. For earlier name, see Nutford Farm in Pimperne to which this farm lies adjacent, with *Locky* from a family here in 13th century. Later name may allude to land held here by French abbey of Fontevrault about same date.

Frankham Farm (in Ryme Intrinseca) *Frankeham* 1244. 'Enclosure of a man called Franca', from an Old English personal name and *hamm*.

French's Farm (in Wimborne St Giles) *Frensshes* 1394. A manorial name, from a family here in the 13th and 14th centuries.

Friar Waddon see Waddon.

Frith House (in Stalbridge) *la Frithe* 1244. From Old English *fyrhth* 'sparse woodland, wooded countryside'.

Frogmore, 'marshy ground frequented by frogs', from Old English *frogga* and *mōr*: (i) **Frogmore Dairy House** (in Toller Porcorum) *Froggemore* 1268. (ii) **Frogmore Hill** (in Chideock) *Frogghemore* 1324.

Frome, River an old Celtic river-name, first recorded in the 9th century and probably meaning 'fair' or 'fine'. Rivers with the same name occur in Somerset, Gloucestershire and Herefordshire. The Dorset river gives its name to four parishes.

Frome Hill (in West Stafford) named from the former manor of Frome Billet (*Frome* 1086 Domesday Book, *Frome Belet* 1268, 'estate on River Frome held by the Norman *Belet* family').

Frome Mead (in Puddletown) *Fromemede* 1325. 'Meadow on River Frome', from Old English *mæd*.

Frome St Quintin *Litelfrome* 1086 (Domesday Book), *Litlefrome* 1202, *Fromequintin* 1288. At first, 'little estate on River Frome', later with affix from the *St Quintin* family, here in 13th century.

Frome Vauchurch *Frome* 1086 (Domesday Book), *Frome Fowechirch* 1288. 'Estate on River Frome with a coloured church', from Old English *fāh* and *cirice*.

Frome Whitfield (in Stinsford) *Frome* 1086 (Domesday Book), *Froma Witefeld* 1243. 'Manor on River Frome of the *de Witefeld* family'. This family was here in the early 13th century.

Fryer Mayne (in West Knighton) *Frarenemayne* 1337, earlier *Mayne Hospitalis* 1244. For Mayne, see under Broadmayne. *Frarene-* ('of the brothers', from Middle English *frere)* and *Hospitalis* ('of the hospital', from the Latin) refer to the Knights Hospitallers who had a preceptory and lands here in 13th century.

Furleigh Farm (in Netherbury) *Ferlegh* 1288. Probably 'clearing where ferns grow', from Old English *fearn* and *lēah*.

Furzebrook (in Church Knowle) thus in 1811, self-explanatory.

Furzehill (in Colehill) *la furshulle* 14th century. Self-explanatory.

Furzey Island (in Poole Harbour) *Fursey* 1545. 'Furze island', from Old English *fyrs* and *ēg,* with later addition of *Island.*

Gallows Hill (in Bere Regis) *Gallis Hill* 1682. A name that speaks for itself, from Old English *galga* and *hyll.*

Galton (in Owermoigne) *Ga(ve)ltone* 1086 (Domesday Book). 'Farm subject to tax or rent', from Old English *gafol* and *tūn.*

Garston Down (in Sixpenny Handley) *La Garston* 15th century. 'The grass enclosure or paddock', from Old English *gærs-tūn.*

Gatemerston (in East Lulworth) *Gatemareston* 1236. Probably 'farm (Old English *tūn*) of a family called *de Gatemore'* (mentioned in 13th century). The surname is from a place-name meaning 'moor where goats are kept', Old English *gāt* and *mōr.*

Gaulter Gap (in Kimmeridge) *Goldehorde* 1451. 'Gold-hoard, treasure of gold', from Old English *gold-hord,* perhaps an allusion to the discovery of a hidden treasure here long ago, although the name could be ironical. The 'gap' refers to a low part of the shore.

Gaunt's Common and House (in Hinton Martell) *the great Gawntz* 1535, *Gantts farme* 1646, probably named from the famous John of Gaunt, Duke of Lancaster 1372-99, who possessed the large manor of Kingston Lacy.

Giddy Green (in Wool) possibly a derogatory name from Middle English *gidi* 'mad, foolish' and *grene.*

Gillingham *Gillinga ham* 11th century (Anglo-Saxon Chronicle), *Gelingeham* 1086 (Domesday Book), *Gillingeham* 1156. 'Homestead of the family or followers of a man called Gylla', from an Old English personal name with *-inga* and *hām.*

Glanvilles Wootton *Widetone* 1086 (Domesday Book), *Wotton Glaunuill* 1288. 'Farm in or by a wood', from Old English *wudu* and *tūn.* Manorial affix from the *Glanville* family, here in 1258.

Goathill *Gatelme* 1086 (Domesday Book), *Gathulla* 1176. 'Hill where goats are pastured', from Old English *gāt* and *hyll.*

Goathorn Plantation and Point (in Studland) *Gotowre* 1286. Probably 'bank or shore where goats are kept', from Old English *gāt* and *ōra,* later *horn* from shape of promontory.

Godlingston Hill and Manor (in Swanage) *Godlington* 1299, *Godelyngston* 1345. 'Farm or estate of a man called Godelin or Godling', from Old English *tūn* and a Middle English personal name.

Godmanstone *Godemanestone* 1166. 'Farm or estate of a man called

Godmann', from an Old English personal name and *tūn*.

God's Blessing Green (in Holt) first recorded as *Godblessing* in 1694, a complimentary name for productive or pleasant land.

Gore, from Old English *gāra* 'triangular plot of land, point of land': (i) **Gore Farm** (in Ashmore) to be associated with *Gore Close, Gores Coppices* 1590. (ii) **Gore Farm** (in Margaret Marsh) *Gora* 1282. (iii) **Gore Heath** (in Wareham) *Gore heathe* 1597.

Gorwell Farm (in Long Bredy) *Gorewull* 1285. 'Dirty spring or stream', from Old English *gor* and *wella*.

Gotham (in Edmondsham) *Goathams* 1838. Probably 'goat enclosure(s)', from Old English *gāt* and *hamm*.

Grange (in Holt) *Graunge* 1327. From Middle English *grange* 'a grange, an outlying farm where crops were stored' .

Grange Farm (in Pulham) so called because there was once a *grange* here (from 13th century) belonging to Bindon Abbey.

Graston (in Burton Bradstock) *Gravstan* 1086 (Domesday Book), *Grauestane* 1210. Old English *stān* 'stone' with either *grāf* 'grove, copse' or *græf* 'grave, pit'.

Great Coll Wood (in Sturminster Marshall) *Colwod* 1284. 'Wood where charcoal was burnt', from Old English *col* and *wudu*, or from Old English *coll* 'hill' with reference to hill spur here.

Great Coombe (in Whitchurch Canonicorum) *Comb* 1332. From Old English *cumb* 'valley'.

Great Ebb (in Symondsbury) *Hebbe* 1329. From Old English *ebba* 'ebb', in the sense 'shore visible at low tide'.

Green Island (in Poole Harbour) only known by this name from 18th century, earlier (from 14th century) *St Helen's Island* (e.g. *Insula Sancte Elene* 1310, from Latin *insula* and *sancta*).

Grim's Ditch (in Pentridge) *Grymesdiche* 1280. 'Ditch associated with Grim', from Old English *dīc*. This is a common name for ancient earthworks such as this one, which crosses the county boundary into Wiltshire. *Grim* is probably a nickname for the heathen Germanic god Woden, to whose activities these earthworks were ascribed (Wansdyke, another earthwork in Wiltshire, is in fact 'Woden's ditch').

Grimstone (in Stratton) *Grimeston* 1212. 'Farm or estate of a man called Grim', from Old English *tūn* and an Anglo-Danish personal name first introduced into England by the Vikings.

Grove (on Isle of Portland) *le Groue* 1323. 'The grove or copse', from Old English *grāf*.

Gulliver's Farm (in West Moors) named from Isaac *Gulliver* 1745-1822.

Gummershay Farm (in Stalbridge) *Gumersheye* 1268. 'Enclosure of a family called Gumer', from Middle English surname and *hæg*.

Gummershay Farm (in Whitchurch Canonicorum) *Gomboldesheye* 1332. 'Enclosure of a family called Gumbald', from Middle English surname and *hæg*.

Guppy (in Wootton Fitzpaine) *Guppehegh* 1254. 'Enclosure of a man called Guppa', from an Old English personal name and *hæg*.

Gussage All Saints *Gyssic* 10th century, *Gessic* 1086 (Domesday Book), *Gersich Omnium Sanctorum* 1155. Probably 'gushing stream', from Old English *gysic* (or from *gyse* and *sīc*), originally the name of the stream rising at Gussage St Andrew. *All Saints* (Latin *Omnium Sanctorum*) is from the dedication of the church.

Gussage St Andrew (in Sixpenny Handley) *Gissic* 877 (15th century copy of Saxon charter), *Gissik St Andrews* 1258. See Gussage All Saints. *St Andrew* from the dedication of the church.

Gussage St Michael *Gessic* 1086 (Domesday Book), *Gyssiche Sancti Michaelis* 1280. See Gussage All Saints. *St Michael* from the dedication of the church. In early times often *Gussiche Dynaunt* or *Bohun*, from families here in 12th and 13th centuries.

Gutch Pool Farm (in Gillingham) *Gowge Pole* 1568. Perhaps from the word *gouge* 'to hollow out', with *pōl* 'pool'.

Guy's Marsh (in Cann) *Gyesmersch* 1401. 'Marshy ground of a man called Guy', from Old English *mersc*.

Half Hide Down (in Farnham) named from *Halueyde* 1288, 'the half hide of land', from Old English *healf* and *hīd*. One of the two manors in Farnham assessed at half a hide in Domesday Book.

Halstock *Halganstoke* 998 (12th century copy of Saxon charter), *Halgestoch* 1212. 'Holy outlying farmstead', from Old English *hālig* and *stoc*, so called because it belonged to the monastery at Sherborne.

Halstock Leigh (in Halstock) *Legh* 1268, from Old English *lēah* 'a wood, a clearing in a wood'.

Ham Common (in Gillingham) named from *Hamme* 12th century. Old English *hamm* 'enclosure, river-meadow'.

Hambledon Hill (in Child Okeford) *Hameledun* 1270. 'The scarred or mutilated hill', from Old English *hamel* and *dūn*, no doubt with reference to the earthworks of the Neolithic causewayed enclosure and Iron Age hill-fort here.

Hambury House and Tout (in West Lulworth) *Hamborough* 1589, *Hanbury* 1597. Possibly 'high hill or barrow', from Old English *hēah* (dative *hēan*) and *beorg*, with *tōte* 'a look out'.

Hamlet (in Yetminster) thus in 1840, from *hamlet* 'small village'.

Hammond Street Farm (in Mappowder) *Hamondes Streete* 1602. From the *Hamond* family, here 1297, and *strete* 'hamlet'.

Hammoon *Hame* 1086 (Domesday Book), *Ham Galfridi de Moiun* 1194, *Hamme Moun* 1280. 'The enclosure or river-meadow of the *Moion* family', from Old English *hamm*. This family, from Moyon in Normandy, already held the manor in 1086.

Hampreston *Hame* 1086 (Domesday Book), *Hamme* 1204, *Hamme Preston* 1244. Originally 'the enclosure or river-meadow', from Old English *hamm* (it is on the River Stour). *Preston* is 'priest farm or estate', Old English *prēost* and *tūn*, probably an allusion to lands here belonging to the College of Wimborne Minster.

Hamworthy (in Poole) *Hamme* 1236, *Hamworthy* 1463. From Old English *hamm* 'enclosure', here possibly used in the sense 'peninsula', with Old English *worthig* also 'enclosure'.

Handfast Point (in Studland) *Handefaste Pointe* 1583. 'High stronghold', from Old English *hēah* (dative *hēan*) and *fæsten*, or 'rock stronghold', from Old English *hān*, perhaps with reference to Studland Castle which was situated on this promontory. Handfast Point is alternatively The Foreland, from *foreland* 'cape, headland'.

Handley see Sixpenny Handley.

Hanford *Hanford* 1086 (Domesday Book), *Haunford* 1228. Probably 'ford at the stone', from Old English *hān* and *ford*. The original ford was on River Stour.

Harbin's Park (in Tarrant Gunville) *parcus de Tarente Gundeuile* 1280, *la Park de Goundevile* 1423, from Middle English *park* (this is the best preserved of Dorset's medieval deer parks), then named from the *Harbin* family who held the manor in the 18th century.

Hargrove Farm (in Stalbridge) *Haregroue, Haregraue* 1268. Possibly 'grove frequented by hares', from Old English *hara* and *grāf,* or the first element may be Old English *hār* 'grey'.

Harley Down (in Gussage All Saints) *Hardeleydune* 1281. 'Hill or down at the hard clearing', from Old English *heard, lēah* and *dūn.*

Harman's Cross (in Worth Matravers) *Armons Cross* 1840, from the surname *Harman* and *cross* 'crossroads'.

Harpitts Farm (in Kington Magna) *Harpete* 1206. 'Grey pit', from Old English *hār* and *pytt.*

Harp Stone, Hurpston (in Steeple) the 'Harp Stone' is situated near Hurpston and both names go back to *Herpere* 1086 (Domesday Book), *Herperston* 1340. Originally 'the harper', from Old English *hearpere,* referring figuratively either to the stone or to the stream here, later with *stān* 'stone' added.

Hartgrove (in East Orchard) *Haregrave* 12th century, *Haregrove* 1450. 'Grove frequented by hares', or 'grey grove', from Old English *hara* or *hār* and *grāf*. Modern -*t*- is quite unhistorical.

Hartland Moor (in Arne) earlier *Harttesknolle* 1545, 'hart's hill-top or hillock', from Old English *heorot* and *cnoll*.

Hartley Farm (in Minterne Magna) *Hertlegh* 1223. 'Wood or clearing frequented by harts', from Old English *heorot* and *lēah*.

Hatherly Farm (in Hilton) *Hetherle* 1227. 'Clearing where hawthorn grows', from Old English *hæg-thorn* and *lēah*.

Hatts Barn (in Ashmore) thus in 1811, cf. *Winsons Hatts* (a coppice) 1618, from Old English *hæt* 'hat-shaped hill' and surname.

Haydon, probably 'hill or down where hay is made', from Old English *hēg* and *dūn* (alternatively from *hege* 'hedge' or *hæg* 'enclosure': (i) **Haydon** (parish) *Heydone* 1163. (ii) **Haydon** (in Lydlinch) *Haydun* 13th century. (iii) **Haydon Hill** (in Charminster) *Haydon* 1617.

Hayes Farm (in Marnhull) *Heis* 16th century. From Old English *hæs* 'brushwood'.

Haythorn (in Horton) *Heythorne* 1551. From Old English *hæg-thorn* 'hawthorn'.

Hayward Bridge (in Child Okeford) *bridge of Hayford* 1268. 'Hay ford', i.e. 'ford used at hay making time', Old English *hēg* and *ford*.

Hazelbury Bryan *Haselber* 1237, *Hasilbere Bryan* 1547. 'Hazel wood', from Old English *hæsel* and *bearu*. Manorial addition from the *Bryene* family (from Brienne in France), here in 14th century.

Heath Farm (in Hampreston) *Heath* 1541. Self-explanatory.

Hemsworth (in Witchampton) *Hemedesworde* 1086 (Domesday Book), *Hemedeswurth* 1243. 'Enclosure of a man called Hemede', from an Old English personal name and *worth*.

Henbury (in Sturminster Marshall) *Hennbyr* 1244, *Hymbury* 1327. Probably 'the high or chief fortified place', from Old English *hēah* (dative *hēan*) and *burh*, or the first element could be Old English *henn* 'water-hen or other wild bird'.

Hengistbury Head (in Bournemouth) *Hedenesburia* 12th century. 'Fortified place associated with a man called Heddīn', from an Old English personal name and *burh*. The later form is due to folk etymology, through association with the 5th-century Germanic chieftain *Hengest* mentioned in the Anglo-Saxon Chronicle.

Heniford Farm (in Melbury Bubb) *Humerford* 1288. 'Ford across a stream called *Humber*', from Old English *ford* and an old river-name (see Hummer) once that of Wriggle River.

Henley (in Buckland Newton) *Henneleghe* 13th century. 'Clearing frequented by hens (of wild birds)', Old English *henn* and *lēah*.

Hermitage *the hermitage of Blakemor* 1309, *Ermytage* 1389. Named from the priory or hermitage founded here in the 13th century.

Herrison (in Charminster) *Harengestun* 1224. 'Manor or estate of the *Harang* family', from Old English *tūn*. This family was here from the early 13th century, and also gave name to Chaldon Herring, Langton Herring and Winterborne Herringston.

Herston (in Swanage) *Herstune* 1086 (Domesday Book), *Her(e)ston* 1288. 'Farm or estate of a man called Here', from an Old English personal name and *tūn*. The man in question actually held part of this manor at the time of Domesday Book.

Hethfelton (in East Stoke) *Elfatune, Hafeltone* 1086 (Domesday Book), *Hethfelton* 1280. 'Farm by the open land overgrown with heather', from Old English *hæth, feld* and *tūn*.

Hewish Farm (in Milton Abbas) *Hywysch* 1385. From Old English *hīwisc* 'measure of land that would support a family'.

Highcliffe (in Christchurch) *Black Cliffe* 1610, *High Clift* 1759.

High Hall (in Pamphill) *High Hall farm* 1663.

High Lea Farm (in Hinton Martell) *High Ley* 1838, from Old English *lēah* 'wood or clearing', also 'meadow'.

High Stoy (in Minterne Magna) *Staweyesfote* 1270, *Stoweye* 1550. 'Stony way', Old English *stān* and *weg*, with *fōt* 'foot (of a hill)' .

Highwood (in East Stoke) *Highwood(s)* 17th century.

Hilfield *Hylfelde* 934 (later copy of Saxon charter), *Hulfeld* 1212. 'Open land by the hill', from Old English *hyll* and *feld*.

Hillamsland (in Hampreston) *Hillamlands* 1553, originally simply called *Hull* 1330, from Old English *hyll* 'hill', with the later addition of *hamm* 'enclosure' and *land* 'estate'.

Hillbutts (in Pamphill) thus in 1811, from *butt* 'archery butt' or *butte* 'short strip ploughed at right angles to others'.

Hillcombe Coppice (in Shillingstone) *Elcombe* 1330. Possibly 'elder-tree valley', from Old English *ellen* and *cumb*.

Hill Farm (in Iwerne Minster) *Hille* 1086 (Domesday Book), *Hulle* 1270. '(Place at) the hill', from Old English *hyll*.

Hilton *Eltone* 1086 (Domesday Book), *Halcton* 1210, *Helton* 1212. From Old English *tūn* 'farm, estate', first element uncertain, possibly Old English *hielde* 'slope', *helde* 'tansy' or *healh* 'nook'.

Hincknoll Hill (in Netherbury) *Hennecnolle* 1288. Probably 'knoll or hillock frequented by wild birds', Old English *henn* and *cnoll*.

Hinton Martell *Hinetone* 1086 (Domesday Book), *Hineton Martel* 1226. 'Estate belonging to a religious community' (probably the former monastery of Wimborne Minster), from Old English *hīwan* (genitive *hīgna*) and *tūn*. Affix from *Martel* family, here in the 13th century.

Hinton Parva *Hynton Parva, Lytlehyneton* 1288. Latin addition *parva* 'little' distinguishes this place from Hinton Martell.

Hinton St Mary *Hamtune* 944 (15th century copy of Saxon charter), *Haintone* 1086 (Domesday Book), *Hinton Marye* 1627. 'High farm, farm situated on high land', Old English *hēah* (dative *hēan*) and *tūn*. Affix is from early possession by the abbey of St Mary, Shaftesbury.

Hoburne (in Christchurch) *Hoburne* 1086 (Domesday Book), *Houburne* 1333. 'Stream by the heel of land', from Old English *hōh* and *burna*.

Hod Hill (in Stourpaine) *Hod* 1270, from Old English *hōd* 'hood' (perhaps an allusion to the shape of the hill) or 'shelter' (with reference to the Iron Age hill-fort crowning it). *Hill* added in 18th century. The fort here may be ancient *Dunium*, see Maiden Castle.

Hogchester (in Wootton Fitzpaine) *Hoggeshurst* 1236, *Hoggescestre* 1427. Probably 'wooded hill where hogs are kept', from Old English *hogg* and *hyrst*, or the first element could be an Old English personal name *Hogg*. The change from *hurst* to *chester* occurs also in Bedchester.

Hogleaze Farm (in Frampton) *Hog(s)lease* 1670. 'Pasture for hogs', from Old English *hogg* and *læs*.

Hogstock (in Tarrant Rushton) *Hogsto(c)ke* 1609. Probably from Old English *stoc* 'an outlying farmstead, a secondary settlement' with either *hogg* 'a hog' or an Old English personal name *Hogg*.

Holcombe Farm (in Alton Pancras) *Holcombe* 1480. 'Deep or hollow valley', from Old English *hol* and *cumb*.

Holdenhurst (in Bournemouth) *Holehest* 1086 (Domesday Book), *Holeherst* 1172, *Holnhurst* 1397. Identical in origin with Holnest.

Holditch Court (in Thorncombe) *Holedich* 1219. 'Hollow ditch', from Old English *hol* and *dīc*.

Holebrook Green (in Lydlinch) *Holambrok* 968 (14th century copy of Saxon charter), *Holebrouk* 1332. 'Hollow brook', i.e. 'brook running in a deep hollow', from Old English *hol* and *brōc*.

Holm and Ivy Farm (in Cann) *la Holmene Theuele* 1341. 'The holly bush or thicket', from a derivative of Old English *holegn* (which gives Dorset dialect *holm*) and *thȳfel*. The modern form is due to folk etymology.

Holmebridge (in East Stoke) *Holmebrygge* 1530. 'Bridge near Holme', with reference to East and West Holme.

Holme, East *Holne* 1086 (Domesday Book), *Estholn* 1288. From Old English *holegn* 'holly tree', 'East' in relation to West Holme.

Holme, West (in East Stoke) *Westholn* 1288. See East Holme.

Holmwood (in Hampreston) dialect *holm* 'holly' (from *holegn*).

Holnest *Holeherst* 1185, *Holenhurst* 1268. 'Wooded hill where holly grows', from Old English *holegn* and *hyrst*.

Holt *Winburneholt* 1185, *Holte* 1372. 'The wood near Wimborne (Minster)', from Old English *holt*. This was a royal chase and forest, recorded as *foresta de Winburne* in 1086 (Domesday Book).

Holt Farms (in Melbury Osmond) *la Holte* 14th century. From Old English *holt* 'wood, thicket'.

Holton (in Wareham) *Holtone* 1086 (Domesday Book), *Holton* 1211. 'Farm in or near a hollow', from Old English *hol* and *tūn*. Or the first element could be Old English *holt* 'wood, thicket'.

Holway Farm (in Cattistock) *Holeweia* 1206. 'Hollow way, way in a hollow', from Old English *hol* and *weg*.

Holwell (parish) *Holewala* 1188, *Holewale* 1201. 'Ridge or bank in a hollow', from Old English *hol* and *walu*.

Holwell (near Broadwey) *Halegewelle* 1086 (Domesday Book), *Halghewell* 1244. 'Holy well, spring or stream', from Old English *hālig* and *wella*.

Holwell Farm (in Cranborne) *Holewella* 1194. 'Hollow stream, stream in a deep valley', from Old English *hol* and *wella*.

Holworth (in Owermoigne) *Holewourthe* 934 (later copy of Saxon charter), *Holverde* 1086 (Domesday Book), *Holewrth* 1204. 'Enclosure in a hollow', from Old English *hol* and *worth*. There is the site of a deserted medieval village here.

Honeybrook Farm (in Holt) *Honybrock* 1300. 'Brook by which honey is found', from Old English *hunig* and *brōc*.

Honeycomb Wood (in Castleton) *Honycombe Wode* 1538. 'Valley where honey is produced', from Old English *hunig* and *cumb*.

Hooke *Lahoc* 1086 (Domesday Book), *Hok* 1209. 'The hook or angle, the land in a river-bend', from Old English *hōc*. River Hooke (earlier *Toller*) has its name from this place, see Tollerford.

Hookswood Farm (in Farnham) *Hookes-Wood* 1774, probably named from *Hoke* 1621, Old English *hōc* 'hook, angle or bend'.

Horn Hill and Park (in Broadwindsor) *Horhulle* 13th century, *Horne hill*, *Horne Park* 1621. Old English *horn* 'horn-shaped hill'.

Horton *Hortun* 1033 (12th century copy of Saxon charter), *Hortune* 1086 (Domesday Book). 'Dirty or muddy farm', Old English *horu* and *tūn*.

Hound Hill (in Pamphill) *Houne Hill* 1591. From Old English *hund* 'hound' or the plant-name *hūne* 'hoarhound'.

Huish, from Old English *hīwisc* 'a household, a measure of land that would support a household': (i) **Huish** (in Winterborne Zelstone) *Hiwysh* 1327. (ii) **Huish Farm** (in Sydling St Nicholas) *Hywyssh* 1280.

Hummer (in Trent) *Humbre* 1106. Named from the small stream here, an ancient pre-English river-name of uncertain origin.

Huntingford (in Gillingham) *Hunteneford* 1258. 'The hunters' ford', from Old English *hunta* (genitive plural *huntena*) and *ford*. This was on the boundary of the royal forest of Gillingham.

Hurn *Herne* 1086 (Domesday Book), *Hurne* 1242. 'The angle or corner of land', from Old English *hyrne*, perhaps originally with reference to the land between Moors River and River Stour.

Hurpston (in Steeple) see Harp Stone.

Hursey (in Burstock) *Herstanesheia* 1201. 'Enclosure of a man called Heorstān', from an Old English personal name and *hæg*.

Hurst (in Moreton) *Herste* 1251. Old English *hyrst* 'wooded hill'.

Hyde, 'the hide of land (originally an amount of land sufficient to support a family)', from Old English *hīd*: (i) **Hyde** (in Bothenhampton) *la Hyde* 1244. (ii) **Hyde Farm** (in Tarrant Hinton) *Hida* 1242, also *Stokehyde* from 15th century, probably from manorial association with East Stoke. (iii) **Hyde Heath and House** (in Bere Regis) *Hyde* 1285.

Hydes (in Lydlinch) *Hydes* 1431. Named from the family of Roger *de la Hide* 1268, from Old English *hīd* as in previous names.

Ibberton *Abristetone* 1086 (Domesday Book), *Hedbredinton* 1212, *Edbrightinton* 1288. 'Farm called after a man named Ēadbeorht', from an Old English personal name and *-ingtūn*.

Iford (in Bournemouth) *Huver* 12th century, *Uvre* 1272. From Old English *yfer* 'a slope'. Alteration to Iford is probably quite recent.

Ilsington (in Puddletown) *Elsangtone* 1086 (Domesday Book), *Ilsington* 1257. Probably 'farm called after a man named Ælfsige', from an Old English personal name and *-ingtūn*.

Innsacre (in Shipton Gorge) *Insaker* 13th century. Probably 'plot of arable or cultivated land of a man called Ine', from an Old English personal name and *æcer*.

Ivy Cross (in Shaftesbury) *Ivy Crosse* 1574. Self-explanatory.

Iwerne, River an old Celtic river-name, probably 'yew river', first recorded in the 10th century and giving its name to three parishes.

Iwerne Courtney or Shroton *Werne* 1086 (Domesday Book), *Yuern Curtenay* 1244, *Schyreuetone* 1337. 'Estate on River Iwerne of the

Courtenay family'; the *Courtenays*, Earls of Devon, were here from 13th century. Alternative name Shroton means 'sheriff's farm or estate', from Old English *scīr-rēfa* and *tūn;* the Domesday Book manor belonged to Baldwin of Exeter, *sheriff* of Devon.

Iwerne Minster *Ywern* 877 (15th century copy of Saxon charter), *Evneminstre* 1086 (Domesday Book). River Iwerne rises here. Addition is Old English *mynster* 'church of a monastery, large church'.

Iwerne Steepleton *Werne* 1086 (Domesday Book), *Stepleton* 1234, *Iwernestapleton* 1346. 'Village on River Iwerne with a church steeple', from Old English *stīepel* and *tūn*.

Jordon Hill (near Preston) *Churdon* 1452. Probably 'hill at the turn or bend', from Old English *cierr* and *dūn*, with reference to the course taken by River Jordon (which is named from the hill).

Jumpers Common (in Christchurch) from a family called *Jumper* recorded in the 16th century.

Kendalls, The (in Gillingham) recorded as two fields called *Kendle* 1839, possibly to be associated with *Kynhull* 1280, 'royal hill' from Old English *cyne-* and *hyll*, or 'cows' hill' from Middle English *kyne*.

Kershay Farms (in Netherbury) *Kyrseheye* 1306. From Old English *hæg* 'enclosure', first element possibly a surname.

Keysworth Farm (in Wareham) *Kaerswurth* 1227. Probably 'enclosure where cress grows', from Old English *cærse* and *worth*. The farm is near River Piddle.

Kimmeridge *Cameric, Cuneliz* 1086 (Domesday Book), *Kimerich* 1212, *Kymerygge* 1489. 'Splendid or convenient track or strip of land', or 'track or strip belonging to a man called Cȳma'. Old English *cȳme* or personal name and *ric*.

King Barrow (in Alderholt) *Kyngbor'ghe* 1404. From Old English *beorg* 'barrow, hill'. This is a natural mound, not a tumulus, so 'king' perhaps alludes simply to its size.

Kingcombe, Higher and Lower (in Toller Porcorum) *Chimedecome* 1086 (Domesday Book), *Kendecumb* 1212. 'Valley where wallgermander grows', from Old English *cymed* and *cumb*.

King Down (in Pamphill) *the Kinges Downe* 1591. It lay within the former royal manor of Kingston Lacy.

King's Court Wood (in Motcombe) named from the former 'King's Court Palace' first recorded in the 13th century and reputed to have been a royal hunting lodge.

Kingsettle Farm (in Motcombe) *Kyngesettl* 1268. Literally 'king's seat', from Old English *cyning* and *setl*, perhaps used as a hill-name since the farm lies on the lower slopes of a hill that reaches 800 feet. Or the name may have referred to a royal hunting lodge or the like in the old forest of Gillingham.

Kingsland (in Netherbury) *Kingesland* 1237. 'Land or estate of a family called *Kyng*', from Old English *land*.

King's Mill Bridge (in Marnhull) *Kingesmolne* 1268. Self-explanatory, from Old English *cyning* and *myln*.

Kingstag (in Lydlinch) *Kingestake* 1337. 'King's stake or boundary post', from Old English *cyning* and *staca*. The boundaries of three parishes meet here on the bridge over River Lydden.

Kingston, 'the king's farm or estate, the royal manor', from Old English *cyning* and *tūn*: (i) **Kingston** (in Corfe Castle) *Chingestone* 1086 (Domesday Book), *Kingeston* 1212. In a Saxon charter dated 948, Eadred king of Wessex granted land here to the abbess of Shaftesbury. (ii) **Kingston** (in Hazelbury Bryan) *Kingeston* 1580. (iii) **Kingston Lacy Hall** (in Pamphill) *Kingestune* 1170, *Kynggestone Lacy* 1319. Manorial affix from John *de Lacy*, earl of Lincoln, to whom the manor was granted in 1230. The present 17th century hall replaced an earlier house. (iv) **Kingston Maurward** (in Stinsford) *Kingeston* 1244, *Kyngeston Marlevard* 1280. Affix from the family of Geoffrey *Mauregard* who is mentioned here in 1247. (v) **Kingston Russell** *Kingeston* 1212, *Kyngeston Russel* 1284. Affix from the family of John *Russel* who held it of the king in 1212.

Kingswood Farm (in Studland) *Kyngeswode* 1397. 'The king's wood', from Old English *cyning* and *wudu*.

Kington Farm, Little (in West Stour) *Chintone* 1086 (Domesday Book), *Parva Kynton* 1238, *Little Kyngton* 1272. 'Little' (Latin *parva*) to distinguish this place from Kington Magna.

Kington Magna *Chintone* 1086 (Domesday Book), *Magna Kington* 1243, *Great Kington* 1290. 'Royal manor', from Old English *cyne-* and *tūn*, with Latin *magna* 'great'.

Kinson *Chinestanestone* 1086 (Domesday Book), *Kynestanton* 1231. 'Farm of a man called Cynestān', Old English personal name and *tūn*.

Kitford Bridge (in Folke) *Kytefordbrygge* 1484. 'Bridge at the ford frequented by kites', from Old English *cȳta, ford* and *brycg*.

Knaps Hill farm (in Buckland Newton) *Knapshill* 1675. Named from the family of Thomas *Cnap*, here in 14th century.

Knighton, 'farm or estate of the young men or retainers', from Old English *cniht* and *tūn*, although in names originating after 1066 *cniht* may have its later sense 'knight': (i) **Knighton** (in Beer Hackett) *Knythteton* 1288. (ii) **Knighton** (in Canford Magna) *Knyghteton* 1288. (iii) **Knighton,**

East (in Winfrith Newburgh) *Knytteton* 1244. (iv) **Knighton House** (in Durweston) *Knicteton* 1212. This manor was held by five thanes or retainers in the 11th century. (v) **Knighton, West** (parish) *Chenistetone* 1086 (Domesday Book), *Cnititon* 1208. This manor was held by two thanes or retainers in 1066.

Knitson Farm (in Langton Matravers) *Knyghtwyneston* 1309. 'Farm or estate of a man called Cnihtwine', from an Old English personal name and *tūn*.

Knob's Crook (in Woodlands) possibly an allusion to the sharply curved ridge here, Middle English *knob* 'knoll' and *crok* 'bend'.

Knoll, '(place at) the hill-top or hillock', from Old English *cnoll*: (i) **Knoll** (in Buckland Newton) *Knolle* 1268. (ii) **Knoll, The** (in Corfe Mullen) *La Cnolle* 1228.

Knowle, Church see Church Knowle.

Knowle Hill (in Woodlands) *Cnolle* 1212, *Knoll-Hill Farm* 1650. From Old English *cnoll* 'hill-top, hillock'; the hill rises to over 250 feet, and gives name to Knowlton.

Knowlton (in Woodlands) *Chenoltune* 1086 (Domesday Book), *Cnolton* 1212. 'Farm by the hillock', from Old English *cnoll* (i.e. Knowle Hill) and *tūn*.

Lackington, White see White Lackington.

Lake Farm (in Thornford) *Lake* 1563. Old English *lacu* 'a stream'.

La Lee Farm (in Winterborne Whitechurch) *la Le* 1244. 'The wood or woodland clearing', Old English *lēah* with French definite article, the survival of which suggests strong French influence (the manor was held in medieval times by Milton Abbey).

Lambrook (in Netherbury) *Lambrok* 1268. 'Brook by which lambs are pastured', from Old English *lamb* and *brōc*.

Landscombe Lane (in Buckland Newton) from *Lemanescombe* 1327, 'lover's valley', from Middle English *leman* and *combe*.

Langbourne (in Langton Long Blandford) not on early record, but no doubt 'long stream' from Old English *lang* and *burna*.

Langdon Farm (in Beaminster) *Langedon* 1244. 'Long hill or down', from Old English *lang* and *dūn*.

Langford Farm (in Stratton) *Langeford* 1086 (Domesday Book). 'Long ford', from Old English *lang* and *ford*. The ford was across Sydling Water, a tributary of River Frome.

Langham (in Gillingham) *Langeham* 1156, *Langenham* 1280. 'The long enclosure or river-meadow', Old English *lang* and *hamm*.

Langton Herring *Langetone* 1086 (Domesday Book), *Langeton Heryng*

1336. 'Long farm or estate', from Old English *lang* and *tūn*. Manorial affix from the *Harang* family, here from 13th century, see Chaldon Herring, Herrison and Winterborne Herringston.

Langton Long Blandford *Bleneford* 1086 (Domesday Book), *Longeblaneford* 1242, *Blaneford Langeton* 1280. Originally distinguished from the other Blandfords by Old English *lang* 'long', then by its alternative name Langton, 'long farm or estate' from Old English *lang* and *tūn*. *Langeton Botiller* and *Langeton Latyle* were early manors here named from two different families.

Langton Matravers *Langeton* 1165, *Langeton Mawtravers* 1428. 'Long farm or estate', from Old English *lang* and *tūn*. Manorial addition from the *Mautravers* family, here from 13th century.

Lankham Bottom (in Cattistock) *Langcum* 1317. 'Long valley', from Old English *lang* and *cumb*.

Laverstock Farm (in Stoke Abbott) *Laurechestocam* 12th century, *Larkestok* 1244. 'Farm frequented by larks', from Old English *lāwerce* and *stoc*.

Lazerton Farm (in Stourpaine) *Werne* 1086 (Domesday Book), *Lazereton* 1270, *Iwernelazerton* 1346. Originally named from River Iwerne on which it stands. Lazerton is possibly 'farm of the leech gatherers', from Old English *læcere* and *tūn*.

Leeson House (in Langton Matravers) *Lesinton* 1224. Probably 'farm called after a man named Lēofsige', from an Old English personal name and *-ingtūn*.

Leigh, 'the wood or woodland clearing', from Old English *lēah*: (i) **Leigh** (parish) *Lega* 1228, *Legh* 1244. (ii) **Leigh** (in Colehill) *Lege* 1086 (Domesday Book), *Leye* 1280.

Leigh Park (in Wimborne Minster) *Leye park* 1348. Named from Leigh in Colehill; there was a medieval deer-park here.

Lenthay (in Sherborne) *Lentehay* 1454. 'Enclosure used at Lent or in Spring', from Old English *lencten* and *hæg*.

Letton (in Pimperne) *Litten* 1784, possibly *Lacton* 1332. Perhaps Old English *lēac-tūn* 'herb garden'.

Lewcombe (in East Chelborough) *Leuecumbe* 1268. 'Sheltered valley', or 'valley with a shelter', Old English *hlēo(w)* and *cumb*.

Lewell Farms (in West Knighton) *Lewelle, Liwelle* 1086 (Domesday Book), *Lywolle* 1285. Probably 'well or spring with a shelter', from Old English *hlēo* or *hlēow* and *wella*.

Lewesdon Hill (in Broadwindsor) *Lewsdown* 1495. Possibly 'hill of a man called Lēofwīg', Old English personal name and *dūn*.

Leweston *Leweston, Leuston* 1244, *Leuweston* 1288. Probably 'farm of a man called Lēofwīg', from an Old English personal name and *tūn*.

Lillington *Lillington, Lullinton* 1200. 'Farm called after a man named Lylla', from an Old English personal name and *-ingtūn*.

Lilliput (in Poole) *Lillypute* 1783. A literary name, like the nearby Branksome. Lilliput is the name of the imaginary country peopled by pygmies in Jonathan Swift's *Gulliver's Travels* (1726). It is probably no coincidence that in the 18th century there was a prominent family in these parts called *Gulliver*!

Lily Farm (in Charmouth) *Lidleghe* 1240. Probably 'woodland clearing with a gate', from Old English *hlid* and *lēah*.

Lim, River see Lyme Regis.

Limbury Farm (in Netherbury) *Lymbury* 1288. 'Lime-tree hill, or where flax is grown', from Old English *lind* or *līn* and *beorg*.

Linton Hill (in Abbotsbury) *Lyndone* 1332. 'Hill or down where flax is grown', from Old English *līn* and *dūn*.

Lions Hill (in St Leonards and St Ives) named from a family called *Lyne*, here in the 16th century.

Littledown (in Bournemouth) *le Lytildoune* 13th century. Self-explanatory, from Old English *dūn* 'hill, down'.

Little Mayne Farm (in West Knighton) *Maine* 1086 (Domesday Book), *Parva Maene* 1202, *Lyttlemayne* 1306. 'Little' (Latin *parva*) to distinguish this manor from Fryer Mayne and Broadmayne.

Littlemoor (in Broadwey) *Lytilmore* 1431. From Old English *lytel* and *mōr* 'moor, marshy ground'.

Little Puddle Farm and Hill (in Piddlehinton) *Litele Pudele* 934 (later copy of Saxon charter), *Pidre* 1086 (Domesday Book). 'Little estate on River Piddle', from Old English *lytel*.

Littleton (in Blandford St Mary) *Liteltone* 1086 (Domesday Book), *Litletun* 1220. 'Little farm or estate', from Old English *lytel* and *tūn*, so named to distinguish it from Langton (Long Blandford) on opposite bank of River Stour.

Littlewindsor (in Broadwindsor) *Windresorie* 1086 (Domesday Book), *Parva Windlesor* 1209, *Little Windesore* 1279. 'Little' (Latin *parva*) to distinguish this manor from Broadwindsor.

Little Wood (in Chettle) *littlen wde* 935 (15th century copy of Saxon charter). Self-explanatory, from Old English *lytel* and *wudu*.

Litton Cheney *Lidinton* 1194, *Lideton, Ludeton* 1204. 'Farm by a torrent or noisy stream', from Old English *hlȳde* and *tūn*. Manorial addition from the *Cheyne* family, here from the late 14th century.

Locketts Farm (in Hazelbury Bryan) *Lockets* 1697. From the family of

John *Locket*, here in late 14th century.

Lodden, River probably an old Celtic river-name, identical in origin with River Lydden; it is first recorded in the 13th century.

Loders *Lodre(s)* 1086 (Domesday Book), *Loddre(s)* 1244. Possibly the old Celtic name of the river here, now called Asker, from *loch* 'pool' and *dour* 'water'. Or from Celtic *lo-dre* 'homestead'.

Lodmoor (near Melcombe Regis) *lodomor* 984 (14th century copy of Saxon charter), *Lodemor* 1297. Possibly 'muddy tract of marshy land', from Celtic *lūta* 'mud' and Old English *mōr*.

Longbury (in Gillingham) *Langborowe* 1609. 'Long barrow', from Old English *lang* and *beorg*.

Longcombe Bottom (in Fontmell Magna) *Langencumb* 932 (15th century copy of Saxon charter). 'Long valley', Old English *lang* and *cumb*.

Longfleet (in Poole) *Langeflete* 1230. 'Long inlet or creek', from Old English *lang* and *flēot*.

Longham (in Hampreston) *Longeham* 1541. 'Long enclosure or river-meadow', from Old English *lang* and *hamm*.

Long Lane Farm (in Holt) *Langlanne* 1524. Self-explanatory.

Longmoor Farm (in Gillingham) *Longmore* 1650. Self-explanatory, from Old English *mōr* 'marshy ground'.

Looke Farm (in Puncknowle) *Luk* 1212. Possibly from an Old English word *lūce* meaning 'enclosure'.

Lorton (in Broadwey) not in early records, but possibly 'dirty farm', from Old English *lorte* and *tūn*.

Loscombe (in Powerstock) *Loscum* 1244. 'Valley with a pig-sty', from Old English *hlōse* and *cumb*.

Loverley Farm (in Gussage All Saints) *Loverlay, Luverlay* 12th century, *Loverlee* 1288. Probably 'wood or clearing of a woman called Lēofwaru', from an Old English personal name and *lēah*.

Lowbrook Farm (in Okeford Fitzpaine) *Lollebrok* 1264. Probably 'brook of a man called Lulla', Old English personal name and *brōc*.

Lox Lane Farm (in Gillingham) *Lockslane* 1599, from a surname *Lock*.

Loxtree Farm (in Evershot) *Lokestrewe* 1268. 'Tree associated with a family called Lok', from Old English *trēow*.

Luccombe Farms (in Milton Abbas) *Loucome* 1317. Probably identical in origin with the next name.

Luccombe Farm (in Netherbury) *Leucom* 1251. 'Sheltered valley', or 'valley with a shelter', Old English *hlēo* or *hlēow* and *cumb*.

Luckford Lake (a tributary of River Frome) *Luggeford* 1381. Possibly 'ford of a man called Lugga', from *ford* and an Old English personal name. Or first element may be an old river-name of Celtic origin.

Lulworth, East and West *Lulvorde, Loloworde* 1086 (Domesday Book), *Westlullewrth* 1258, *Estlolleworth* 1268. 'Enclosure of a man called Lulla', from an Old English personal name and *worth*.

Luscombe Valley (in Poole) *Loscomb* 1822. 'Valley with a pig-sty', from Old English *hlōse* and *cumb*.

Luton Farm and Down (in Tarrant Monkton) *(Tarante) Loueton* 1280. Probably 'farm (on River Tarrant) of a man called Lufa', from an Old English personal name and *tūn*. *Tarrant* was only finally dropped from the name in the 17th century.

Lutton (in Steeple) *Lutteton* 1288. 'Farm of a man called Lutta', from an Old English personal name and *tūn*.

Lydden, River an old Celtic river-name, first recorded in the 10th century and probably meaning 'the broad one', see Lydlinch.

Lydford Farm (in Cann) *Glideford* 1280. 'Ford frequented by the kite or other bird of prey', from Old English *glida* and *ford*. Initial *G-* is lost from the 16th century.

Lydlinch *Lidelinz* 1182, *Lidelinch* 1285. 'Ridge by, or bank of, River Lydden', from Old English *hlinc*.

Lymburgh's Farm (in Marnhull) *Linberg, Limberghe* 1244. Either 'lime-tree hill' from Old English *lind* and *beorg,* or 'hill where flax is grown' if the first element is Old English *līn*.

Lyme Regis *Lim* 774 (12th century copy of Saxon charter), *Lime, Lym* 1086 (Domesday Book), *Lyme Regis* 1285. Like Uplyme in Devon named from River Lim, an old Celtic river-name meaning simply 'stream'.

Lynch Farm (in Corfe Castle) *hlinc* 956 (14th century copy of Saxon charter), *La Linche* 1254. 'The ridge or bank', from Old English *hlinc*.

Lyscombe Farm (in Cheselbourne) *Liscombe* 934 (later copy of Saxon charter), *Liscome* 1086 (Domesday Book). 'Valley where reeds grow', from Old English *lisc* and *cumb*.

Lytchett Matravers *Lichet* 1086 (Domesday Book), *Lichet Mautrauers* 1280. An old Celtic name meaning 'grey wood' from Celtic *lēd* and *cēd*. The woodland here is mentioned in Domesday Book. Manorial addition is from the family of Hugh *Maltrauers* who held the manor in 1086, see Langton Matravers.

Lytchett Minster *Licheminster* 1244, *Lechet Ministre* 1269. For the meaning of Lytchett, see Lytchett Matravers. Minster is from Old English *mynster* 'large church', probably with reference to the church at Sturminster Marshall, of which Lytchett Minster was once a chapelry.

Madjeston (in Gillingham) *Malgereston* 1205, *Maugereston* 1266. 'Farm of a man called Malger', from Old English *tūn* and a Continental Germanic personal name.

Magiston Farm (in Sydling St Nicholas) *Magereston* 1330. Probably identical in origin with previous name.

Maiden Castle (in Winterborne St Martin) *Mayden Castell* 1607. The same name is applied to a number of other prehistoric earthworks in Britain besides this Iron Age hill-fort. The meaning may be 'fortification thought never to have been taken, one that looks impregnable', or simply refer to the fact that this was a place frequented by girls, a lovers' haunt. Maiden Castle is possibly the city of *Dunium* (from Celtic *dūno* 'a fort') referred to by the Greek geographer Ptolemy in the 2nd century, but this is more likely the fort at Hod Hill.

Maiden Newton *Newetone* 1086 (Domesday Book), *Maydene Neweton* 1288. 'New farm', from Old English *nīwe* and *tūn*. The addition means 'of the maidens', from Old English *mægden;* the exact allusion is obscure, but it could suggest that the manor was once owned by nuns.

Main Down (in Tarrant Gunville) *la Menedon* 1397. 'The common hill or down', from Old English *mæne* and *dūn*.

Mandeville Stoke Farm (in Whitchurch Canonicorum) *Stoches* 1086 (Domesday Book), *Stok Maundeuyl* 1288. Old English *stoc* 'secondary settlement', with later manorial addition from the *Mandeville* family, here from 12th century. In early times often called *Stoke Waleys,* so named from another family.

Mangerton (in Netherbury) *Mangerton* 1207, *Mangereston* 1274. 'Farm of the traders or merchants', from Old English *mangere* and *tūn*.

Mannington (in Holt) *Manitone* 1086 (Domesday Book), *Maninton* 1244. 'Farm called after a man named Mann or Manna', from an Old English personal name and *-ingtūn*.

Manor Farm (in Motcombe) earlier called Woodsend Farm, *Wodesende* 13th century, 'end of the wood'.

Manor Hill (in Tarrant Gunville) *Manewodehulle* 1397. 'Hill at the common wood', from Old English *mæne, wudu* and *hyll*.

Manston *Manestone* 1086 (Domesday Book), *Manneston* 1196. 'Farm of a man called Mann', Old English personal name and *tūn*.

Manswood (in Moor Crichel) *Mangewood* 1774. Perhaps from the word *mange* 'cutaneous disease of animals caused by a parasite'.

Mappercombe Manor (in Powerstock) *Mepercumbe* 1285. From Old English *cumb* 'valley', first element uncertain.

Mapperton (parish) *Ma(l)peretone* 1086 (Domesday Book), *Mapeldoreton* 1236. 'Maple-tree farm', from Old English *mapuldor* and *tūn*.

Mapperton (in Sturminster Marshall) *Mapeldertune* 943 (15th century copy of Saxon charter), *Mapledretone* 1086 (Domesday Book). Identical in origin with the previous name.

Mappowder *Mapledre* 1086 (Domesday Book), *Mapoldre* 1189, *Maupodre* 1227. From Old English *mapuldor* 'a maple-tree'.

Margaret Marsh *Margaretysmerschchurche* 1395, *Margret marshe* 1575. Self-explanatory, from Old English *mersc* 'marsh'. *Margaret* may be from the dedication of the church, or the name of an early owner of the estate, as in nearby Guy's Marsh. Since it belonged to Shaftesbury Abbey, the *Margaret* in question may have been one of the two 14th century abbesses so named.

Marley Wood (in Winfrith Newburgh) *Muryle* 1390. 'Pleasant wood or clearing', or 'wood or clearing where merry-making took place', from Old English *myrge* and *lēah*.

Marnhull *Marnhulle* 1267, *Marenhull* 1274, *Marnell* 1426. From Old English *hyll* 'hill', first element uncertain. It may be an Old English personal name *Mearna,* or an Old English noun *mearn* referring to the soft stone or marl found here.

Marshalsea (in Marshwood) *Mareschalesheighes* 1344. 'Enclosure(s) of a family called *Mareschal*', from Old English *hæg*.

Marsh, from Old English *mersc* 'marsh': (i) **Marsh Farm** (in Bloxworth) *Mersch* 1327. (ii) **Marsh Farm** (in Ibberton) *le Merche* 1327. (iii) **Marsh Farm** (in Stalbridge) *the Mersch* 1327.

Marshwood *Merswude* 1188, *Mershwod* 1288. 'Wood by a marsh', from Old English *mersc* and *wudu*. This place gives its name to Marshwood Vale, first recorded in the 14th century (*Merswodeuaal* 1319), from Middle English *vale* 'a wide valley'.

Martinstown see Winterborne St Martin.

Matravers (in Loders) *Lodre* 1086 (Domesday Book), *Lodres Luttone* 1285, *Lodres Mautravers* 1356. For original name, see Loders. Earlier addition *Luttone* is from Litton Cheney (through some manorial connection). Later addition *Mautravers* is from the family of this name, here c.1300.

Matterley Cottages (in Woodlands) *mapoldor lea* 1033 (12th century copy of Saxon charter), *Materlie* 1551. 'Maple-tree wood or clearing', from Old English *mapuldor* and *lēah*.

Maumbury (in Dorchester) *Memburi* 1333, *Mambury, Maumbiry* 1382, *Malmebury* 1553. From Old English *burh,* here in the sense 'pre-English earthwork' since Maumbury is a 'henge monument' of Neolithic date which later served as a Roman amphitheatre. First element uncertain, possibly Old English *mealm* 'sandy or chalky soil' or Old English *mæne* 'common' or Celtic *main* 'rock or stone'.

Meerhay (in Beaminster) *Merheye* 1327. 'Enclosure by a pool', from Old English *mere* and *hæg*.

Melbury Abbas *Meleburge* 956 (14th century copy of Saxon charter), *Meleberie* 1086 (Domesday Book), *Melbury Abbatisse* 1291. Probably 'multi-coloured fortified place', from Old English *mæle* and *burh*. Addition is a reduced form of Latin *abbatissa* 'abbess', since this manor, like Compton Abbas, belonged to Shaftesbury abbey from 956.

Melbury Bubb *Meleberie* 1086 (Domesday Book), *Melebir Bubbe* 1244. One of a group of names in the west of the county identical in origin with Melbury Abbas. Manorial addition from the *Bubbe* family, here from the early 13th century.

Melbury Osmond *Melesberie* 1086 (Domesday Book), *Meleberi Willelmi filii Osmundi* 1202, *Melebur Osmund* 1283. See Melbury Bubb. The addition is manorial, from the 'William son of Osmund' who presumably held this manor in or before 1202. The dedication of the church here to St Osmond must have come later.

Melbury Sampford *Meleberie* 1086 (Domesday Book), *Melebury Saunford* 1312. See Melbury Bubb. Manorial affix from the *Saunford* family here from the late 13th century. In early times often called *Melbury Turberville*, from the family of that name.

Melcombe Bingham see Bingham's Melcombe.

Melcombe Horsey *Melecumb* 1205, *Melcombe Horsey* 1535. Probably 'milk valley', i.e. 'valley where milk was produced, fertile valley', from Old English *meoluc* and *cumb*. Manorial addition from the *Horsey* family, here in the 16th century. In early times often called *Upmelcombe* or *Overmelcombe* (*up*- 'upper', *over*- 'higher') to distinguish it from Bingham's Melcombe.

Melcombe Regis *Melecumb* 1223, *Melcoumbe Regis* 1336. Identical in origin with Melcombe Horsey. Melcombe was anciently royal demesne, hence Latin *regis* 'of the king'.

Melplash (in Netherbury) *Melpleys* 1155, *Melepleisch* 1312. Probably 'multi-coloured pool', from Old English *mæle* and *plæsc*.

Merritown (in Hurn) *Merry town alias Funk Town* 1682, earlier *Fonketon* 14th century. *Merry town* may be ironical (from Old English *myrge* 'pleasant'), since *Fonketon* may be from Middle English *fonke* 'a spark (of fire)', perhaps alluding to a smithy.

Merry Field Hill (in Colehill) *Meriefelde* 1595. 'Pleasant field' or 'field where merry-making took place', Old English *myrge* and *feld*.

Middlebere Farm and Heath (in Arne) *Middlebere* 1291. 'Middle wood or woodland pasture', Old English *middel* and *bearu* or *bær*.

Middlemarsh (in Minterne Magna) *Middelmersh* 1227. Self-explanatory, from Old English *middel* and *mersc.*

Milborne St Andrew *Muleburne* 934 (later copy of Saxon charter), *Meleburne* 1086 (Domesday Book), *Muleburne St Andrew* 1294. Named from the stream on which it stands, 'mill stream', from Old English *myln* and *burna. St Andrew* from dedication of church to distinguish it from Milborne Stileham.

Milborne Stileham *Meleburne, Meleborne* 1086 (Domesday Book), *Muleburn* 1258, *Milborn Stylam* 1431. Named from the same stream as Milborne St Andrew. Stileham may be a place-name meaning 'enclosure at the stile or steep ascent', Old English *stigel* and *hamm.* In early times also called *Milborne Bek,* from its possession by Benedictine abbey of Bec-Hellouin in Normandy.

Mill Down (in Pimperne) *Mulledoune* 1382. Self-explanatory.

Milton Abbas *Middeltone* 934 (later copy of Saxon charter), *Mideltune* 1086 (Domesday Book), *Middelton Abbatis* 1268. 'Middle farm or estate', from Old English *middel* and *tūn.* The addition is Latin *abbas* 'an abbot', with reference to the abbey here.

Milton on Stour (in Gillingham) *Mideltone* 1086 (Domesday Book), *Milton on Stoure* 1397. Identical in origin with Milton Abbas, 'middle' perhaps alluding to its position between Gillingham and Silton. It is on the River Stour.

Milton, West (in Powerstock) *Mideltone* 1086 (Domesday Book), *Midelton* 1212. *West* to distinguish it from Milton Abbas.

Minchington (in Sixpenny Handley) *Munecheneton* 1307. 'Farm belonging to the nuns', from Old English *myncen* and *tūn*, alluding to the possession of this manor by the Benedictine nunnery of Shaftesbury. In medieval times this place was often known as 'Gussage Minchington' from its proximity to Gussage St Andrew.

Minterne Magna & Parva *Minterne* 987 (13th century copy of Saxon charter), *Minterne Parva* 1314, *Great Mynterne* 1363, *Mynterne Magna* 1596. 'House at the place where mint grows', from Old English *minte* and *ærn*, with Latin *magna* 'great' and *parva* 'small'.

Miz Maze (in Leigh) thus in 1774, from *mizmaze* 'maze, labyrinth'.

Mogers Leaze (in Clifton Maybank) *Mogers lease* 1563. Old English *læs* 'pasture', with surname of the local *Moger* family.

Monastery Farm (in East Lulworth) so called because originally built in 1795 as a monastery for some refugee Trappist monks.

Monkton Up Wimborne (in Wimborne St Giles) *Winburne* 1086

(Domesday Book), *Vpwimburn Abbatis* 1268, *Wymborne Monkton* 1504. For *Up* and *Wimborne,* see Wimborne St Giles. *Monkton* is 'estate of the monks' from Old English *munuc* and *tūn,* alluding to possession by abbey of Tewkesbury (Latin *abbatis* 'of the abbot').

Monkton Wyld see Wyld Farms (in Wootton Fitzpaine).

Monkwood, 'wood belonging to the monks', from Old English *munuc* and *wudu:* (i) **Monkwood** (in Marshwood) *Munkewode* 1244, with reference to possession by Sherborne abbey. (ii) **Monkwood Hill Farm** (in Piddletrenthide) *Munkewode* 1244, probably with reference to the monks of Glastonbury Abbey.

Monmouth's Ash (in Woodlands) in a field called *Monmouths Field* in 1840, named from the Duke of Monmouth, illegitimate son of Charles II, who was captured hiding in an ash-tree here (no longer standing) after his defeat at the battle of Sedgemoor in 1685.

Moorbath (in Symondsbury) *Mordaat* 1086 (Domesday Book), *Morba* 1200, *Morbath* 1244. 'Bathing-place or pool in marshy ground', from Old English *mōr* and *bæth.*

Moor Court Farm, Moorside (in Marnhull) *Mora* 13th century, *Moorecorte alias Mooreside* 1597. Old English *mōr* 'moor, marshy ground', with the later addition of *court* 'manor house' and *side* 'side'.

Moorcourt Farm (in Sturminster Marshall) *Moreis* 1204, *Moors Court* 1346. 'Manor house of a family called *More*', from *court.*

Moor Crichel see Crichel.

Moordown (in Bournemouth) *Mourdon* late 13th century, *Mourden* 1300. Probably identical in origin with Morden.

Moors River a recent name, from East and West Moors.

Morcombelake (in Whitchurch Canonicorum) *Mortecumb* 1240, *Morecomblake* 1558. Probably 'valley of a man called Morta', from an Old English personal name and *cumb,* with *lacu* 'stream'.

Morden *Mordune, Mordone* 1086 (Domesday Book), *Mourdone* 1340. 'Hill in marshy ground', from Old English *mōr* and *dūn.* The two manors of East and West Morden are recorded from 13th century.

Moreton *Mortune* 1086 (Domesday Book), *Moreton* 1195. 'Marshland farm', from Old English *mōr* and *tūn.*

Mosterton *Mortestorne* 1086 (Domesday Book), *Mortesthorn* 1209. 'Thorn-tree of a man called Mort', from an Old English personal name and *thorn.*

Motcombe *Motcumbe, Motecumb* 1244, *Mottecumbe* 1288. 'Valley where meetings are held', from Old English *mōt* and *cumb.* Probably meeting-place of old medieval hundred of Gillingham.

Mount Ararat (in Verwood) remote hill on Boveridge Heath named after mountain on which Noah's ark is said to have rested!

Muckleford (in Bradford Peverell) *Mukelford* 1244. 'Ford of a man called Mucela', from an Old English personal name and *ford*. The ford was across River Frome.

Mude, River a late back-formation from Mudeford.

Mudeford (in Christchurch) *Modeford* 13th century. 'Muddy ford', from Middle English *mode, mudde* 'mud' and *ford*.

Mupe Bay and Rocks (in West Lulworth) *Mewup hill* 1753, *Muop's Bay* 1774. Perhaps 'small bay frequented by seagulls', from Old English *mæw* and *hōp*.

Muscliff (in Bournemouth) *Museclive* 1242. 'Cliff or slope infested with mice', from Old English *mūs* and *clif*.

Muston Farm (in Piddlehinton) *Mostereston* 1270. 'Estate of the *de Musters* family', from Old English *tūn,* see Winterborne Muston.

Mythe Hill (in Mapperton) *Methe* 1423. From Old English *mȳthe* 'a confluence of rivers'.

Nash, '(place at) the ash-tree', from Old English *æsc*, with initial *N-* from Middle English *atten* 'at the': (i) **Nash Court** (in Marnhull) *Asshe* 1347, *Aysshcourt* 1482, *Naishe* 16th century. (ii) **Nash Farm** (in Marshwood) *Nayssh* 1351. This was no doubt the home of Roger *Attenasshe* 1319.

Netherbury *Niderberie* 1086 (Domesday Book), *Nitherbury* 1285. 'Lower fortified place', from Old English *neotherra* and *burh*.

Netherhay (in Broadwindsor) *Netherhey* 1244. 'Lower enclosure', Old English *neotherra* and *hæg*, contrasting with a lost *Uphay*.

Netherstoke (in Halstock) *Nitherstoc* 1145. 'Lower outlying farmstead', from Old English *neotherra* and *stoc*, 'lower' in relation to Halstock.

Nettlecombe (in Powerstock) *Netelcome* 1086 (Domesday Book). 'Valley where nettles grow', from Old English *netel* and *cumb*.

New Cross Gate (in Shillingstone) from *cross* 'cross-roads'.

Newland (in Glanvilles Wootton) *Newelond* 1396. 'Land newly cleared and brought into cultivation', Old English *nīwe* and *land*.

Newlands Farm (in Batcombe) *Neulond* 1274. See previous name.

New Mills Heath (in Corfe Castle) *Neumulle* 1334. 'The new mill(s)', from Old English *nīwe* and *myln*. The Corfe River is nearby, but there is no mill now.

Newnham Farms (in Broadwindsor) *Newenham* 1227. 'New enclosure', from Old English *nīwe* (dative *nīwan*) and *hamm*.

Newton, 'new farm or estate', from Old English *nīwe* and *tūn*: (i) **Newton** (in Studland) *Nyweton* 1404. In 1286 there was an ambitious proposal to start a 'new town' here, but it was probably never more than a tiny hamlet. (ii) **Newton** (in Sturminster Newton) see Sturminster Newton. (iii) **Newton Farm** (in Hilton) *Niwton, Newton* 1400. (iv) **Newton Farm** (in Lytchett Minster) *Niweton* 1332. (v) **Newton Peveril** (in Sturminster Marshall) *Neuton* 1260, *Neweton Peverel* 1306. Manorial affix from the *Peverel* family, here in the 13th century, see Bradford Peverell.

New Town (in Witchampton) site of a new village built in the late 18th century to rehouse the displaced inhabitants of Moor Crichel.

Norden Farm and Heath (in Corfe Castle) *Northdon* 1291. 'North hill or down', from Old English *north* and *dūn*.

Normandy Farm (in Winterborne Stickland) perhaps commemorating possession of a manor here in 1086 (Domesday Book) by Norman abbey of Coutances, but probably a name of recent origin.

Norris Mill (in Puddletown) recorded 1625, from the *Norris* family.

Northbourne (in Bournemouth) a recent name for a modern district of the town, contrasted with Southbourne and Westbourne.

Northbrook (in Puddletown) *Bynorthebrouk* 14th century. '(Place) to the north of the brook', from Old English *northan* and *brōc*.

North Haven Point (in Poole) *Northavensford* 1341, *Northe Havyn Poynt* 1539. From Old English *hæfen* 'harbour'; it is opposite South Haven Point, at the entrance to Poole Harbour. It is clear from the 14th century spelling that there was once a ford here where there is now a ferry.

North Hayes Farm (in Motcombe) *le Northhey* 1317, *Northayes* 1501. 'Northern enclosure(s)', from Old English *north* and *hæg*.

Northport (in Wareham) *Northeport* 1370. Probably '(place) to the north of the town', from Old English *northan* and *port*.

Northwood Farm (in Manston) *Northwode* 1332. Self-explanatory, from its situation at the northern end of the parish.

Nothe, The (in Weymouth) *Waymouthe Northe* 1604. From Old English *hnoth* 'knoll, hill', as in White Nothe which is also a coastal promontory.

Nottington (in Broadwey) *Notinton* 1212. 'Farm called after a man named Hnott or Hnotta', from OE *-ingtūn* and personal name.

Notton (in Maiden Newton) *Natton* 1288, *Netton* 1289. 'Cattle farm', from Old English *nēat* and *tūn*.

Nutford Farm (in Pimperne) *Nortforde* 1086 (Domesday Book), *Nutteford* 1228. 'Ford where nuts grow', from Old English *hnutu* and *ford*; the ford is over River Stour. In medieval times sometimes *Blakenotford*, 'black, dark', probably to distinguish it from *Notfordlocky*, now France Farm.

Nyland (in Kington Magna) *Iland* 1086 (Domesday Book), *Nilonde* 1581.

'The island, the dry ground in marsh', from Old English *īeg-land*, with initial *N*- from Middle English *atten* 'at the'.

Oakers Wood (in Affpuddle) *Wolgariswode* 1465. 'Wood of a man called Wulfgār', from Old English personal name and *wudu*.

Oakford Farm (in Marshwood) *Okford* 1268. 'Oak-tree ford', from Old English *āc* and *ford*.

Oakley, 'oak-tree wood or clearing', from Old English *āc* and *lēah*: (i) **Oakley** (in Canford Magna) *Ocle* 1327. (ii) **Oakley Down and Farm** (in Wimborne St Giles) *ac lee* 956 (14th century copy of Saxon charter), *Ockeleghe* 1280.

Oborne *Womburnan* 975 (12th century copy of Saxon charter), *Wocburne* 1086 (Domesday Book), *Woburn* 1212. '(Place at) the crooked or winding stream', from Old English *wōh* and *burna*.

Ogden Down Farm (in Gussage St Michael) *Hocken Down* 1842. 'Sheep down', from plural of dialect *hogg* 'young sheep'.

Okeford, Child *Acford* 1086 (Domesday Book), *Childacford* 1227. 'Oak-tree ford', from Old English *āc* and *ford*, one of a group of three parishes which share this name, the others being Okeford Fitzpaine and Shillingstone (earlier called *Okeford Shillyng*). Affix may be from Old English *cild* 'young nobleman' (perhaps genitive plural *cilda* 'of the young noblemen'), or from *cielde* 'a spring'.

Okeford Fitzpaine *Acford* 939-46, *Adford* (for *Ac-*) 1086 (Domesday Book), *Ocford Fitz Payn* 1321. See Child Okeford. Manorial affix from family of *Fitz Payn*, here from the 13th century, see Wootton Fitzpaine. Also called *Acford Alvredi* or *Aufrey* from earlier possession by the famous Alvred de Lincoln.

Old Harry (in Studland) a chalk sea-stack recorded thus in 18th century, *old harry* being a familiar name for the devil. A second sea-stack known as Old Harry's Wife collapsed in 1896.

Old Lawn Farm (in Pamphill) *Old Land* 16th century, probably referring to 'formerly used, or long used, arable land'.

Orchard, East and West (parishes) *Archet* 939 (15th century copy of Saxon charter), *Orchet* 1330, *West Orchard* 1427, *Estorchard* 1575. '(Place) beside the wood', from Celtic *cēd* 'wood' with *ar* 'beside, facing'.

Orchard, East and West (in Church Knowle) *Horcerd* 1086 (Domesday Book), *Orcharde* 1291. 'The orchard', from Old English *orceard*. The orchard here is noted in Domesday Book.

Organ Ford (in Lytchett Minster) *Argent* 1194, *Organforde* 1593, *Orgayne alias Organt* 1600. Probably a name of French origin transferred from Argent in the French department of Cher.

Osehill Green (in Glanvilles Wootton) *Oswaldeshulle* 1270. 'Hill of a man called Ōsweald', Old English personal name and *hyll*.

Osmington *Osmyntone, Osmingtone* 934 (later copies of Saxon charters), *Osmentone* 1086 (Domesday Book). 'Farm called after a man named Ōsmund', Old English *-ingtūn* and personal name.

Overcombe (in Preston) 'higher valley', from *cumb*.

Ower (in Corfe Castle) *Ore* 934 (later copy of Saxon charter), *Oure* 1316. '(Place at) the bank or shore', from Old English *ōra*. This place on the shore of Poole Harbour was once a quay for the shipping of stone.

Owermoigne *Ogre* 1086 (Domesday Book), *Our* 1219, *Oure Moyngne* 1314. Probably 'the wind-gap(s)' from a Celtic *ogrodrust-*, referring to gaps in the chalk hills funnelling winds off the sea. The manor was held by the *Moigne* family from 1212.

Pallington (in Affpuddle) *Palinton* 1244, *Palyngton* 1316. 'Farm called after a man named Pælli', from Old English *-ingtūn* and an Old English personal name.

Pamphill *Pamphilla* 1168, *Pemphull* 1323. From Old English *hyll* 'hill', possibly with an Old English personal name *Pampa* or *Pempa*, or with a word *pamp* also 'hill'.

Park Farm (in Gillingham) named from a medieval deer park within the royal forest here (recorded from early 13th century).

Park Farm (in Marshwood) *la Parroc* 13th century. From Old English *pearroc* 'a small enclosure, a paddock'.

Parkstone (in Poole) *Parkeston* 1326. 'The park stone', probably with reference to a stone marking the boundary of a medieval deer park, from Middle English *park*.

Parley, East (in Hurn) *Est Purle* 1280. See next name.

Parley, West *Perlai* 1086 (Domesday Book), *Westperele* 1305. 'Wood where pear-trees grow', from Old English *peru* and *lēah*, with *west* to distinguish it from East Parley.

Parnham (in Beaminster) *Perham* 1228, *Perhamme* 1413. 'Pear-tree enclosure or river-meadow', from Old English *peru* and *hamm*. Spelling with *-n-*, first found in 15th century, is unhistorical.

Parrett, River see Perrott.

Paynthouse Farm (in Cann) not recorded before 19th century, probably from *penthouse* 'an outhouse or shed with sloping roof'.

Peacemarsh (in Gillingham) *Pesemershe* 1535. 'Marshy land where peas are grown', from Old English *pise* and *mersc*.

Pegg's Farm (in Iwerne Minster) *Pegges* 1346. Named from the family of John and Robert *le Peg* who had lands here in 1317.

Penbury Knoll (in Pentridge) recorded from 18th century, the name for the summit of Pentridge Hill. From Celtic *penn* 'hill', Old English *burh* (with reference to hill-fort here) and *cnoll* 'hill-top'.

Pen Hill (in Sutton Waldron) earlier *Seaxpenn* 932 (15th century copy of Saxon charter), 'hill of the Saxons', from Old English *Seaxe* and Celtic *penn*. The hill may have marked an ancient Saxon boundary. It was also an old hundred meeting place, giving its name *Sexpene* to a Domesday Book hundred that was later combined with Handley hundred to form the hundred of Sixpenny Handley. 'Sixpenny' is from *Sexpene* through folk etymology, see Sixpenny Farm and Sixpenny Handley.

Penn (in Wootton Fitzpaine) *la Penne* 1244. From Celtic *penn* 'hill' or Old English *penn* 'pen, enclosure for animals' .

Pentridge *Pentric* 762 (13th century copy of Saxon charter), *Pentric* 1086 (Domesday Book), *Pentrich* 1264. Probably 'the hill of the boar', from Celtic *penn* and *tyrch* (genitive of *twrch* 'boar'). The hill referred to is Pentridge Hill which rises to 600 feet.

Perrott, South *Pedret* 1086 (Domesday Book), *Suthperet* 1268. Named from River Parrett, a Celtic name, 'stream with four fords'. *South* to distinguish this place from North Perrott in Somerset.

Perry Copse and Farm (in Alderholt) *Purie* 1324. 'The pear-tree', from Old English *pyrige*.

Petersham Farm (in Holt) *Pitrichesham, Petrishesham* 1086 (Domesday Book), *Piterichesham* 1263. 'Homestead or enclosure of a man called Peohtrīc', from Old English *hām* or *hamm* and a personal name.

Peveril Point (in Swanage) from 1539, the surname *Peverel*.

Philliols Farm (in Bere Regis) *Pillols* 1617. Named from the *Piliol* family, in this area from the 14th century.

Picket Farm (in South Perrott) *Pikyate* 1236. 'Gate or pass by a pointed hill', from Old English *pīc* and *geat*.

Piddle, River from Old English *pidele* 'a marsh, a fen'. Recorded from 10th century and giving name to six parishes. The discrepancy between *Piddle-* and *Puddle-* in these names reflects alternative spellings for the river-name even in very early times, and one is not really more 'correct' than the other, but for local sensitivity on the matter, see Puddletown. Alternative name Trent (only from 16th century) probably arose through a misunderstanding of the name Piddletrenthide.

Piddlehinton *Pidele* 1086 (Domesday Book), *Hinepidel, Pidel Hineton* 1244. 'Estate on River Piddle belonging to a religious community', from Old English *hīwan* (genitive *hīgna*) and *tūn*. It belonged to the French abbey of Marmoutier in late 11th century.

Piddles Wood (in Sturminster Newton) *Putteleswurthe* 13th century. 'Enclosure of the hawk, or of a man called Pyttel', from Old English *pyttel* or an Old English personal name and *worth*.

Piddletrenthide *Uppidelen* 966 (15th century copy of Saxon charter), *Pidrie* 1086 (Domesday Book), *Pidele Trentehydes* 1212. 'Estate on River Piddle assessed at thirty hides' (its assessment in Domesday Book), from Old French *trente* 'thirty' and Old English *hīd* 'a hide of land', with *up* 'higher upstream' in earliest spelling.

Pilford (in Hampreston) *Pilforde* 1583. Probably 'ford marked by a stake', from Old English *pīl* and *ford*.

Pilsdon *Pilesdone* 1086 (Domesday Book), *Pillesdun* 1168. Probably 'hill of the peak, peaked hill', from Old English *pīl* and *dūn*, with reference to Pilsdon Pen, at 909 feet the highest hill in Dorset (Pen is Celtic *penn* 'hill' or Old English *penn* 'enclosure').

Pimperne *Pimpern* 935 (15th century copy of Saxon charter), *Pinpre* 1086 (Domesday Book). Meaning uncertain. Perhaps a Celtic name meaning 'five trees' from *pimp* 'five' and *prenn* 'tree', or of Old English origin, 'place among hills', from a derivative of a word *pimp* 'hill', or 'house at a hill' from Old English *pimp* and *ærn*.

Pinford (in Castleton) *Pinefort* 1160, *Pinford* 1264. From Old English *ford* 'a ford'. First element may be Old English *pīn* 'pine-tree', *pinn* 'pin or peg', or an Old English personal name *Pinna*.

Pipsford Farm (in Corscombe) *Pippeseia* 1197. 'Well-watered land of a man called Pipp', Old English personal name and *ēg*.

Pistle Down (in Edmondsham) thus in 1811, possibly from *epistle* referring to a reading from scriptures during beating the bounds.

Pithouse Farm (near Hurn) *Pyttehouse* 1544. Self-explanatory.

Pitt Farm (in Whitchurch Canonicorum) *la Putte* 1240. From Old English *pytt* 'a pit or quarry'.

Plumber Manor (in Lydlinch) *Plumbere* 1086 (Domesday Book). 'Wood where plum-trees grow', Old English *plūme* and *bearu*.

Plush (in Piddletrenthide) *Plyssch*, *Plissh* 891 (14th century copy of Saxon charter), *Plys* 1268. From Old English *plysc* 'a pool'.

Pokesdown (in Bournemouth) *Pokesdoune* 1300. Probably 'hill or down haunted by a puck or goblin', Middle English *poke* and *doun*.

Poole *Pole* 1183, *la Pole* 1220, *la Poule* 1347. 'The pool or creek', from Old English *pōl*, with reference to Poole Harbour.

Poorton, North and South *Powrtone, Pourtone* 1086 (Domesday Book), *Northportun, Suthporton* 1288. Old English *tūn* 'farm, estate' with an obscure first element for which see Powerstock.

Portesham *Porteshamme* 1024 (Saxon charter), *Portesham* 1086 (Domesday Book). 'Enclosure belonging to the market town', from Old English *port* and *hamm*, no doubt with reference to Abbotsbury.

Portland, Isle of *Port* 9th century (Anglo-Saxon Chronicle), *Portlande* 862 (14th century copy of Saxon charter). 'Land or estate attached to *Port* ('the harbour')', from Old English *port* and *land*. The Bill of Portland, the tapering southern promontory, is mentioned from 1649 and is from Old English *bile* 'a bill, a beak'.

Potterne Farm (in Verwood) *Poterne* 1280, *Wymbourne Poterne* 1384. 'Building where pots are made, a pottery', from Old English *pott* and *ærn*. Addition *Wymbourne* from Monkton Up Wimborne.

Poundbury Camp (in Dorchester) *Ponebury* 1333. Probably 'pre-English earthwork associated with a man called Pūna', from an Old English personal name and *burh*. This is an Iron Age hill-fort.

Povington (in Tyneham) *Povintone* 1086 (Domesday Book), *Povington* 1285. Probably 'farm called after a man named Pēofa', from an Old English personal name and *-ingtūn*.

Powerstock *Povrestoch* 1086 (Domesday Book), *Pourstoke* 1195. From Old English *stoc* 'secondary settlement, outlying farmstead'. The first element, which this name shares with North and South Poorton, is obscure, although it may be an old river-name.

Poxwell *Poceswylle* 987 (13th century copy of Saxon charter), *Pocheswelle* 1086 (Domesday Book). Possibly 'steeply rising ground of a man called Poca', from Old English *swelle* and a personal name, or 'spring of a man called Poc', from Old English *wella* and a different personal name.

Poyntington *Ponditone* 1086 (Domesday Book), *Puntintuna* 1122. 'Farm or estate called after a man named Punt', from an Old English personal name and *-ingtūn*.

Preston, 'priest farm, farm of the priests', from Old English *prēost* and *tūn*: (i) **Preston** (parish) *Prestun* 1228. This was an old prebend of Salisbury cathedral. (ii) **Preston Farm** (in Tarrant Rushton) *Prestetune* 1086 (Domesday Book), *Preston Tarente* 1280. On the River Tarrant. (iii) **Preston Hill and House** (in Iwerne Minster) *Prestone* c.1120.

Puckstone (in Studland) 'goblin's stone', Middle English *poke*.

Puddletown *Pitretone* 1086 (Domesday Book), *Pideleton* 1212, *Pudeleton* 1280. 'Farm or estate on River Piddle', from Old English *tūn*. The name was the subject of local controversy in 1956, when Dorset County Council unsuccessfully sought to change it to Piddletown. Fierce local protest against the change won the day.

Pulham *Poleham* 1086 (Domesday Book), *Puleham* 1130. 'Homestead or enclosure by the pools or streams', from Old English *pull* or *pōl* with either *hām* or *hamm*.

Pulston Barn (in Charminster) *Cerna Pulli* 1166, *Pulleinston* 1236. 'Manor or estate (on River Cerne) of the *Pulein* family', from Old English *tūn*. This family was here from the mid-12th century.

Puncknowle *Pomacanole* 1086 (Domesday Book), *Pomecnolle* 1268. Probably 'hill-top or hillock of a man called Puma', from an Old English personal name and *cnoll*.

Purbeck, Isle of *Purbicinga* 948 (15th century copy of Saxon charter), *Porbi* 1086 (Domesday Book), *Purbik* 1221. 'Beak-shaped ridge frequented by the bittern or snipe', from Old English *pūr* and *bic*. The name originally referred to the prominent central chalk ridge which crosses Purbeck from west to east. In the earliest spelling *-inga* is from Old English *-ingas* meaning 'dwellers in'.

Purcombe, 'pear-tree valley', from Old English *pyrige* and *cumb*: (i) **Purcombe** (in Marshwood) *Pirecumbe* 1220. (ii) **Purcombe Farm** (in Whitchurch Canonicorum) *Pirecumbe* 1244.

Purewell (in Christchurch) *Perewull* 1300. 'Spring or stream by the pear-tree', from Old English *peru* and *wella*.

Purse Caundle see Caundle.

Pussex Farm (in Hurn) perhaps to be identified with *Possochulle* 14th century, from Old English personal name and *hyll*.

Putton (in Chickerell) *Podinton* 1237, *Pudington* 1288. 'Farm called after a man named Puda', from an Old English personal name and *-ingtūn*.

Pymore (in Allington) *Pimore* 1236. 'Marshy ground infested with gnats or other insects', from Old English *pīe* and *mōr*.

Quarleston Farm (in Winterborne Stickland) *Winterburn Quarel* 1232, *Quarellyston* 1268. Originally 'estate on River Winterborne held by the *Quarel* family', here in 13th and 14th centuries, with Old English *tūn*.

Queen Oak (in Bourton) *Queene Oake Close* 1609. No doubt named from one of the Queens of England who at different dates possessed the manor of Gillingham.

Radipole *Retpole* 1086 (Domesday Book), *Redpole* 1166, *Radepol, Radipol* 1237. 'Reed pool', from Old English *hrēod* and *pōl*, with reference to Radipole Lake.

Rampisham *Ramesham* 1086 (Domesday Book), *Rammesham* 1238. Probably Old English *hamm* 'enclosure, river-meadow'. First element uncertain, either Old English *ramm* 'a ram', or a personal name *Ramm*, or Old English *hramsa* 'wild garlic'.

Ranston (in Iwerne Courtney) *Iwerne* 1086 (Domesday Book), *Iwerne*

Randelleston 1257. 'Randulf's manor or estate (on River Iwerne)', from Old English *tūn* and a Norman French personal name.

Rawlsbury Camp (in Hilton) *Raulesbury* 1400. Perhaps 'Radulf's fortification', from Old English *burh* and a Continental Germanic personal name. This is an Iron Age hill-fort.

Redcliff Farm (in Arne) *Radeclive* 1256, *Redclyffe* 1545. '(Place at) the red cliff', from Old English *rēad* and *clif*.

Red Hill (in Bournemouth) from 18th century, self-explanatory.

Rempstone Hall (in Corfe Castle) *Rameston* 1280. Probably 'farm where wild garlic grows', from Old English *hramsa* and *tūn*.

Renscombe Farm (in Worth Matravers) *Hreminescumbe* 987 (13th century copy of Saxon charter), *Romescumbe* 1086 (Domesday Book). 'Valley of the raven, or of a man called Hremn', from Old English *hremn* or personal name and *cumb*.

Revels Inn Farm (in Buckland Newton) *the land of Rivell* 1264. From a family called *Ryvel* here in the 13th and 14th centuries.

Rew (Hill and Manor) (in Winterborne St Martin) *La Rewe* 1283. 'The row (of houses or trees)', from Old English *ræw*.

Ridge, from Old English *hrycg* 'a ridge or bank, a long narrow hill': (i) **Ridge** (in Arne) *Rygge* 1431. (ii) **Ridge** (in Hazelbury Bryan) recorded from 16th century. (iii) **Ridge Cliff** (in Chideock) named from *La Rhigge* 13th century, *Chidiock Rygge* 1495. (iv) **Ridge Farm** (in Wootton Fitzpaine) *Rugge* 1431. (v) **Ridge Hill** (in Buckland Newton) *La Rigge* 14th century.

Ridgeway Hill (in Bincombe) first recorded in 1680, named from the Roman road between Dorchester and Weymouth.

Ringmoor (in Turnworth) *Hringmere* early 13th century. 'Pool near the circular enclosure', from Old English *hring* (referring to one of the ancient earthworks north of the village) and *mere*.

Ringstead Bay (in Owermoigne) named from the lost medieval village of Ringstead in Osmington, *Ringestede* in 1086 (Domesday Book), from Old English *hring* 'ring' and *stede* 'place or site'. The 'ring' was perhaps a stone circle, or a circular enclosure.

Rockley (in Poole) *Rodeclyve* 1341, *Redecliue* 1364. 'Reedy bank', from Old English *hrēod* and *clif*. For development, see Catsley.

Rodden (in Abbotsbury) *Raddun* 1221. 'Red hill or down', from Old English *rēad* and *dūn*. The soil here is a rich red clay.

Rodmore Farm (in Lydlinch) *Rodmor* 1318. 'Moor or marshy ground where reeds grow', from Old English *hrēod* and *mōr*.

Rollington (in Corfe Castle) *Ragintone* 1086 (Domesday Book), *Radelinton*

1236. Probably 'farm called after a man named Rædel', from an Old English personal name and -*ingtūn*.

Romford (in Edmondsham) *Runford* 1268, *Rungeford* 1308. 'Ford marked by a pole or poles', from Old English *hrung* and *ford*.

Rushmore Farm (in Cranborne) *Rushmore* 1620. 'Marshy ground where rushes grow', from Old English *rysc* and *mōr*.

Rushton (in East Stoke) *Riston* 1086 (Domesday Book), *Risshton* 1313. 'Farmstead where rushes grow', Old English *rysc* and *tūn*.

Ryall (in Whitchurch Canonicorum) *Rihull* 1240. 'Hill where rye is grown', from Old English *ryge* and *hyll*.

Ryme Intrinseca *Rima* 1160, *Ryme* 1229, *Ryme Intrinsica* 1611. Old English *rima* 'a rim, an edge, a border', referring to its situation on the county boundary. Latin addition *intrinseca* 'inner, within the bounds' to contrast with former manor of Ryme Extrinseca in Long Bredy.

St Alban's or St Aldhelm's Head (in Worth Matravers) *the foreland of Seynt Aldem* 1500, *Sainct Aldelmes Point* 1543. Named from the small Norman chapel on this promontory, dedicated to St Aldhelm, first bishop of Sherborne.

St Andrew's Farm (in West Lulworth) *Lulleworth St Andrew* 1302. There was once a church here dedicated to St Andrew.

St Catherine's Hill (near Hurn) near a ford on River Stour called *Catelineford* in the 14th century, from *Cateline,* an old French form of Catherine. *Saint* in the modern name is a recent addition.

St Ives *Iuez* 1167, *Yvetis* 1212. Probably from Old English *īfet* 'clump of ivy, place overgrown with ivy'. *Saint* was only added in recent times, partly from association with St Leonards, partly no doubt on the model of the St Ives in Cornwall and Cambridgeshire.

St James (in Shaftesbury) *parochia Sancti Jacobi* 1297, *the paryshe of Sayncte James* 1566. From the dedication of the church here, *James* usually being written *Jacobus* in Latin documents.

St Leonards named from a medieval religious house or hospital dedicated to St Leonard and first recorded in 1288 as *domus Sancti Leonardi de Russeton* 'the house of St Leonard at *Russeton'*. The exact whereabouts of *Russeton* ('rush farm' from Old English *rysc* and *tūn*) is not known but it was probably near River Crane.

St Leonard's Bridge and Farm (in West Moors) named from the religious house of St Leonard, see previous name.

Salterns (in Poole) *Salterns* 1811. From Old English *salt-ærn* 'a building where salt is made or sold'.

Salwayash (in Netherbury) *Shouleweye* 1332, *Shallways Ash* 1682.

'Hollow or narrow way', from Old English *scofl* and *weg*, with -*ash* from former manor of Ash in Netherbury.

Sandbanks (in Poole) first recorded about 1800, self-explanatory. Earlier *ground called Cales* 1579, from the surname *Cale*.

Sandford, 'sandy ford', from Old English *sand* and *ford*: (i) **Sandford** (in Wareham) *Sanford* 1606. (ii) **Sandford Orcas** *Sanford* 1086 (Domesday Book), *Sandford Horscoys* 1372. Manorial affix from *Orescuils* family, here from 12th century.

Sandhills (in Holwell) *Sandhulle* 13th century. Self-explanatory, from Old English *sand* and *hyll*.

Sandley (in Gillingham) *Sandhull* 1292, *Sandehull* 1329, *Sandley* 1609. 'Sandy hill', from Old English *sand* and *hyll*. The change of *hill* to *ley* is due to the lack of stress on the second element.

Sandpit (in Broadwindsor) *Sandpitte* 1244. Self-explanatory, from Old English *sand* and *pytt*.

Sandsfoot Castle (in Weymouth) *Sandfot castel* 16th century, *the Castell of Sandysfoote* 1553. 'Castle at the foot of the sandy shore'.

Sandway (in Bourton) *Sandweye* 1292. Self-explanatory, from Old English *sand* and *weg*.

Seaborough *Seveberge* 1086 (Domesday Book), *Seuenbergh* 1306. 'Seven hills or barrows', from Old English *seofon* and *beorg*.

Seacombe Cliff (in Worth Matravers) *Secombe* 1306. 'Valley opening on to the sea', from Old English *sæ* and *cumb*.

Seatown (in Chideock) *Setowne* 1469, *Zetowne* 1508. 'Farm or estate by the sea', from Old English *sæ* and *tūn*. The spelling with Z- represents a local dialect pronunciation.

Shade House Farm (in Stour Provost) *Shardehowse* 1570. 'House at a cleft or gap', from Old English *sceard* and *hūs*.

Shaftesbury *Sceaftesburi* 877 (15th century copy of Saxon charter), *Sceftesberie* 1086 (Domesday Book). Possibly 'fortified place of a man called Sceaft', from Old English *burh* and an Old English personal name. Or the first element may be Old English *sceaft* 'shaft, pole', used either of some actual pole or figuratively of the prominent steep-sided hill on which the town stands.

Shapwick *Scapeuuic* 1086 (Domesday Book), *Shepwyk* 1238. 'Sheep farm', from Old English *scēap* and *wīc*.

Shatcombe Farm (in Beaminster) *Shotecumbe* 1306. 'Valley by the steep slope(s)', from Old English *scēot* and *cumb*.

Shatcombe Farm (in Wynford Eagle) *Shapcumbe* 1473. 'Valley where sheep are kept', from Old English *scēap* and *cumb*.

Shave, from Old English *sceaga* 'a small wood, a copse': (i) **Shave Cross** (in Marshwood) *la Shaghe* 1220. With later *cross* 'cross-roads'. (ii) **Shave Hill** (in Buckhorn Weston) *Shawe* 1647.

Sherborne *Scireburnan* 864 (12th century copy of Saxon charter), *Scireburne* 1086 (Domesday Book). '(Place at) the bright or clear stream', from Old English *scīr* and *burna*.

Sherborne Causeway (in Motcombe) *Sherbourne causeway* 1568. From Middle English *cauce* 'raised way across marshy ground', this being part of the road from Shaftesbury to Sherborne.

Sherford (in Morden) *Sireford* 1244, *Shyreford* 1311. 'Bright or clear ford', from Old English *scīr* and *ford*.

Shillingstone *Alford* (an error for *Acford)* 1086 (Domesday Book), *Akeford Skelling* 1220, *Shillyngeston* 1444. Originally sharing its name with Child Okeford and Okeford Fitzpaine, later distinguished from them by the name of the man who held the manor at the time of Domesday Book, one *Schelin*. Shillingstone is 'Schelin's estate', from Old English *tūn*.

Shilvinghampton (in Portesham) *Scilfemetune, Silfemetone* 1086 (Domesday Book), *Shelfhamton* 1253. 'Farm of the dwellers by the shelf or slope', from Old English *scylf, hæme* and *tūn*.

Shipstal Point (in Arne) *Shepstall* 1586. 'The sheepfold', from Old English *scēap* and *stall*.

Shipton Gorge *Sepetone* 1086 (Domesday Book), *Scepton* 1268, *Shipton Gorges* 1594. 'Sheep farm', from Old English *scēap* and *tūn*. Manorial addition from family of Ralph *de Gorges,* here from late 13th century. In early times also called *Shipton Maureward,* from another family with lands here in early 13th century.

Shitterton (in Bere Regis) *Scetre* 1086 (Domesday Book), *Schitereston* 1285, *Shyterton* 1332. 'Farm at the stream used as a sewer', from Old English *scitere* and *tūn*. For reasons of prudishness the name is now Sitterton on current maps.

Shroton see Iwerne Courtney.

Silkhay Farm (in Netherbury) *Selkeheye* 1332. 'Enclosure of a family called *Selk',* from Old English *hæg*.

Silton *Seltone* 1086 (Domesday Book), *Salton* 1268, *Silton* 1332. Probably 'farm where sallows or willows grow', from Old English *sealh* and *tūn*.

Simene, River *Simen* 1577. Formed from the name Symondsbury.

Sitterton, see Shitterton.

Sixpenny Farm (in Fontmell Magna) see Pen Hill.

Sixpenny Handley *Hanlee* 877 (15th century copy of Saxon charter), *Hanlege* 1086 (Domesday Book), *Sexpennyhanley* 1575. 'The high wood or clearing', from Old English *hēah* (dative *hēan*) and *lēah*. Note that -*d*-only appears in 15th century, and that 'Sixpenny' is first added in 16th century (from the name of the hundred of Sixpenny Handley, see Pen Hill in Sutton Waldron).

Slait Barn (in Silton) from Old English *slæget* 'a sheep pasture'.

Slape House (in Netherbury) *Slepa* 1226, *Slepe* 1263. From Old English *slæp* 'a slippery, muddy place'.

Slaughtergate Farm (in Gillingham) from *Slaunders Yate* 1609, Old English *geat* 'gate' and a surname. Modern form due to folk etymology and popular association of this place with the slaughter of the Danish Vikings at the battle of Penselwood in 1016.

Sleep Bottom and Brook (in Alderholt) probably from Old English *slæp* 'a slippery, muddy place', with *botm* 'valley'.

Sleight, from Old English *slæget* 'a sheep pasture': (i) **Sleight** (in Corfe Mullen) *Sleyte* 1327. (ii) **Sleight Buildings** (in Winfrith Newburgh) *Sleight* 1641.

Slepe, 'the slippery, muddy place', from Old English *slæp*: (i) **Slepe** (in Arne) *Slepe* 1244. (ii) **Slepe** (in Lytchett Minster) *Slape* 1315.

Small Mouth (in Wyke Regis) *Smalemue* 1244, *Smalemouth* 1328. 'The narrow mouth', from Old English *smæl* and *mūtha,* alluding to the estuary of East Fleet. There was a ferry here across to Isle of Portland until 1839 when the bridge called Ferry Bridge was built.

Smedmore Hill and House (in Kimmeridge) *Metmore* 1086 (Domesday Book), *Smethemore* 1242. 'Smooth or level moor', Old English *smēthe* and *mōr*. The Domesday Book spelling is erratic.

Smetherd Farm (in Fifehead Neville) *Smitheard* 1744. Perhaps 'smithy yard', from Old English *smethe* and *geard.*

Snelling Farm (in Turners Puddle) *Snellyng* 1415. 'Place of a man called Snell', from an Old English personal name and -*ing.*

Snow's Down (in Langton Long Blandford) from the family of George *Snow* who held the manor in the 18th century.

Somerford (in Christchurch) *Sumerford* 12th century. 'Ford (on River Mude) used only in summer', Old English *sumor* and *ford.*

Sopley Common (in Hurn) named from Sopley in Hampshire, *Sopelie* 1086 (Domesday Book), 'wood or clearing of a man called Soppa', from an Old English personal name and *lēah.*

Southbourne (in Bournemouth) like Northbourne and Westbourne, a name of recent invention for a district of the town.

Southbrook (in Bere Regis) *Suthebrok* 1300. '(Place to) the south of the brook', from Old English *sūthan* and *brōc.* The brook is that which gives name to Shitterton.

Southcombe Valley (in Piddletrenthide) *Suthcombe* 1557. 'South valley', from Old English *sūth* and *cumb*.

South Down Farm (in Owermoigne) *Suddon* 1327, *Sooden Farme* 1664. 'South hill or down', from Old English *sūth* and *dūn*.

South Haven Point (in Studland) *Sowthe Havyn Poynte* 1539. See North Haven Point (in Poole).

Southover, 'south bank', from Old English *sūth* and *ōfer*: (i) **Southover** (in Frampton) *Southover* 1670, with reference to River Frome. (ii) **Southover Heath and House** (in Tolpuddle) *Southouere* 1400, probably with reference to River Piddle.

Southwell (on Isle of Portland) *Southwelle* 1608. 'South spring or stream', from Old English *sūth* and *wella*.

Sovell Down (in Gussage St Michael) probably to be associated with *La Southfelde* 1367, from Old English *feld* 'open country'.

Spetisbury *Spehtesberie, Spesteberie* 1086 (Domesday Book), *Spectesbury* 1294. 'Pre-English earthwork frequented by the green woodpecker', from Old English *speoht* and *burh*. Or the first element is the same word used as a personal name. The reference is to Crawford Castle or Spetisbury Rings, an Iron Age hill-fort.

Springbourne (in Bournemouth) a name of recent invention for a district of the town.

Stafford, West *Stanford, Staford* 1086 (Domesday Book), *Stafford* 1212, *West Stafford* 1285. 'Stony ford', from Old English *stān* and *ford*, alluding to a crossing of River Frome. There was formerly an East Stafford in the neighbouring parish of West Knighton.

Stake Ford Cross (in Yetminster) *Stakyforde* 1350, *Stakeford* 1398. 'Ford marked out by stakes', from Old English *staca* and *ford*. The stakes perhaps marked the boundary between the three parishes that meet here.

Stalbridge *Stapulbrige* 860-6 (14th century copy of Saxon charter), *Staplebrige* 1086 (Domesday Book), *Stapelbrigge* 1212. 'Bridge built on posts or piles', from Old English *stapol* and *brycg*.

Stalbridge Weston (in Stalbridge) *Westtune* 933 (12th century copy of Saxon charter), *Westone* 1086 (Domesday Book). 'West farmstead or estate', from Old English *west* and *tūn*. *Stalbridge* (from the parish) was added to the name in the 17th century.

Stallen (in Nether Compton) *Stawell* 1244, *Stanwell* 1290. '(Place at) the stony spring or stream', from Old English *stān* and *wella*.

Stanbridge (in Hinton Parva) *Stanbrig* 1230. 'Stone bridge', from Old

English *stān* and *brycg,* although *brycg* here may have alternative sense 'causeway, raised track through marshy ground', since Wimborne road crosses low-lying land by River Allen here.

Stanbridge Mill Farm (in Horton) named from a medieval stone bridge across River Allen, called in Latin *pontem petre* in 1280, and *la Stanebrigge* in 1311, from Old English *stān* and *brycg.*

Stancombe Farm (in Litton Cheney) *Stancombe* 1337. 'Stony valley', from Old English *stān* and *cumb.*

Stanpit (in Christchurch) *Stanpeta* 1086 (Domesday Book), *Stanputta* 12th century. 'Stone pit', from Old English *stān* and *pytt.*

Stanton St Gabriel *Stantone* 1086 (Domesday Book), *Staunton Gabriell* 1434. 'Stone-built farmstead, or farmstead on stony ground', Old English *stān* and *tūn.* St Gabriel from the dedication of the church.

Stapehill (in Hampreston) *Staphill* 1583. Apparently 'steep hill', from Old English *stēap* and *hyll;* since there is only a low hill here, the name is possibly ironical.

Steeple *Stiple* 1086 (Domesday Book), *Stuple* 1204, *Stepel* 1222. 'Steep place', from Old English *stīepel.* The word can also mean 'steeple, tower' but the topographical meaning is more likely here.

Steepleton Iwerne see under Iwerne.

Sterte (in Poole) *Strette* 1520, *Stert* 1822. Probably from Old English *steort* 'tail of land'.

Stinsford *Stincteford* 1086 (Domesday Book), *Stinteford* 1236, *Stintesford* 1244. 'Ford frequented by the sandpiper or dunlin', from Old English *stint* and *ford.*

Stoborough (in Arne) *Stanberge* 1086 (Domesday Book), *Stabergh* 1253. 'Stony hill or barrow', from Old English *stān* and *beorg.* Second element has been replaced by *burh* 'fortification' .

Stockbridge Farm (in Lillington) *Stokbrigg* 1244. 'Bridge made of logs', from Old English *stocc* and *brycg.*

Stock Gaylard House (in Lydlinch) *Stoches* 1086 (Domesday Book), *Stok* 1268, *Stoke Coilard* 1305, *Stoke Gaillard* 1316. 'Outlying farm buildings, secondary settlement', from Old English *stoc.* Affix probably manorial, from a family called *Coilard.*

Stock Hill (in Gillingham) neighbouring places are *Stokkefeld* 1441, *Stokford* 1501, *Stock waye* 1626. All are from Old English *stocc* 'tree-stump' or *stoc* 'secondary settlement'.

Stock Hill (in Glanvilles Wootton) *Stochullane* 1441. '(Lane by) hill where there are tree-stumps', Old English *stocc, hyll* and *lane.*

Stockley Farms (in Bere Regis) *Stocle* 1308, *Stockley* 1403. 'Clearing with tree-stumps', from Old English *stocc* and *lēah*.

Stockwood *Stocwode* 1223, *Stokwud* 1224. 'Wood belonging to a secondary settlement', from Old English *stoc* and *wudu*. Earlier often called *Stoke St Edwold* from the dedication of the church.

Stoke Abbott *Stoche* 1086 (Domesday Book), *Stok Abbatis* 1273, *Stoke Abbots* 1275. 'Secondary settlement of the abbot', from Old English *stoc*. It belonged to the abbey of Sherborne (Latin *abbatis* 'of the abbot').

Stoke, East *Stoches* 1086 (Domesday Book), *Stok* 1284, *Estok* 1316. 'Outlying farm buildings, secondary settlement', from Old English *stoc*. 'East' perhaps in relation to Bindon Abbey in Wool.

Stokeford (in East Stoke) *Stokford* 1244. 'The ford near Stoke'.

Stoke Wake *Stoche* 1086 (Domesday Book), *Stok* 1212, *Stoke Wake* 1285. Old English *stoc* 'secondary settlement, outlying farmstead'. Affix is from the *Wake* family, here in the 13th century.

Stone (in Pamphill) *la Stane* 1268, from Old English *stān* 'a stone', perhaps originally with reference to a boundary stone.

Stour, River an Old English river-name, first recorded in the 10th century and probably meaning 'the strong or powerful one'. Rivers with the same name occur in several other counties. The Dorset river gives its name to East and West Stour, Stourpaine, Stour Provost, Sturminster Marshall and Sturminster Newton,

Stour, East and West *Sture* 1086 (Domesday Book), *Sturewestouere* 1268, *Stoure Estouere* 1371. Named for their situation on River Stour. The earlier additions *Estouere* and *Westouere* mean 'east bank' and 'west bank', from Old English *ōfer*. In medieval times these places were sometimes known as *Stour Cosin* and *Stour Wake*, from two families who had lands here.

Stourpaine *Sture* 1086 (Domesday Book), *Sture Payn* 1280. 'Estate on River Stour held by the *Payn* family', here in 13th and 14th centuries.

Stour Provost *Stur* 1086 (Domesday Book), *Sture Preauus* 1270, *Stowr Provost* 1549. Named from River Stour. Early affix is from abbey of St Leger at *Preaux* in Normandy which held manor in 12th to 13th centuries. It was changed to *Provost* after manor was given by Edward IV to the Provost of King's College Cambridge.

Stourton Caundle *Candel(le)* 1086 (Domesday Book), *Caundelhaddon* 1275, *Stourton Candel* 1709. For the name Caundle, see Bishop's Caundle. Affix *Stourton* is from the Lords *Stourton* who held the manor from the 15th century. Earlier affix from *Haddon* family, here in 1202.

Stratton *Stratton* 1212, *Stratone* 1270. 'Farm on a Roman road', from Old English *stræt* and *tūn*. The Roman road from Dorchester to Ilchester was joined here by a branch from Stinsford.

Stro(u)de, from Old English *strōd* 'marshy land overgrown with brushwood': (i) **Strode** (in Netherbury) *Strode* 1225. (ii) **Stroud Bridge** (in Bloxworth) named from *Stroda* 1303. (iii) **Stroud Farm** (in Lydlinch) *Stroude* 1340.

Stubhampton (in Tarrant Gunville) *Stibemetune* 1086 (Domesday Book), *Stubhamtune* 1262. Probably 'farm of the dwellers by the tree-stumps', from Old English *stybb, hǣme* and *tūn*. In medieval times often *Tarente Stubhampton* because River Tarrant rises here.

Studland *Stollant* 1086 (Domesday Book), *Stodland* 1210. 'Tract of land where a herd of horses is kept', Old English *stōd* and *land*.

Sturminster Marshall *Sture minster* 9th century (11th century copy of Saxon charter), *Sturminstre* 1086 (Domesday Book), *Sturministre Marescal* 1268. 'The church on the River Stour', from Old English *mynster*. The manorial addition is from the *Marshals,* earls of Pembroke, of whom William *Mareschal* was here in 1204.

Sturminster Newton *Nywetone, at Stoure* 968 (14th century copy of Saxon charter), *Newentone* 1086 (Domesday Book), *Sturminstr Nyweton* 1291. Newton is 'new farm or estate', from Old English *nīwe* and *tūn,* Sturminster is 'church on River Stour', from Old English *mynster.* Newton (on opposite side of river to Sturminster) was added to name to distinguish this place from Sturminster Marshall.

Sturthill, Higher and Lower (in Shipton Gorge) *Sterte* 1086 (Domesday Book), *Stertel* 1212, *Upsteortel* 1268, *Nithersturtel* 1329. From Old English *steortel* 'projecting or pointed piece of land'.

Sugar Hill (in Bloxworth) not on early record, but possibly 'hill frequented by robbers', from Old English *scēacere* and *hyll.* The name applies to a stretch of road crossing Bloxworth Heath.

Sutton Holms (in Wimborne St Giles) *Suddon* 1226, *Suthdun* 1241, *Sutton Holms* 1811. 'South hill or down', from Old English *sūth* and *dūn. Holms* is from Dorset dialect *holm* 'holly'.

Sutton Poyntz (near Preston) *Suttone* 891 (14th century copy of Saxon charter), *Sutone* 1086 (Domesday Book), *Sutton Pointz* 1314. 'South farm or estate', from Old English *sūth* and *tūn.* The manor was held by the *Poyntz* family from the 13th century.

Sutton Waldron *Suttune* 932 (15th century copy of Saxon charter), *Sudtone* 1086 (Domesday Book), *Sutton Walerand* 1297. 'South farm or estate', from Old English *sūth* and *tūn,* 'south' perhaps in relation to Fontmell Magna. Affix from *Waleran* the huntsman, who held this manor at the time of Domesday Book.

Swalland Farm (in Kimmeridge) *Swanlond* 1376. 'Land or estate of the herdsmen or peasants', from Old English *swān* and *land*.

Swanage *Swanawic* 9th century (Anglo-Saxon Chronicle), *Swanwic* 1086 (Domesday Book), *Swanwyche* 1244. Probably 'dairy farm of the herdsmen or peasants', from Old English *swān* and *wīc*. Or from Old English *swan* 'a swan', thus 'farm where swans are reared, swannery'.

Swineham (in Wareham) *Swynham* 1650. Probably 'water-meadow where swine are kept', from Old English *swīn* and *hamm*.

Swyre, from Old English *swēora* 'a neck of land, a col': (i) **Swyre** *Svere* 1086 (Domesday Book), *Swere* 1196. (ii) **Swyre Head** (in Chaldon Herring) thus in 1811, with *head* 'headland'. (iii) **Swyre Head** (in Corfe Castle) *swuren* 955 (14th century copy of Saxon charter), *Swyer hill* 1590.

Sydling St Nicholas *Sidelyng* 934 (17th century copy of Saxon charter), *Sidelince* 1086 (Domesday Book), *Brodesideling* 1288. '(Place at) the broad ledge or ridge', from Old English *sīd* and *hlinc*. *Brodesideling* ('broad') to distinguish it from Up Sydling. Later affix from dedication of church.

Sydling, Up (in Sydling St Nicholas) *Upsidelinch* 1230, with *Up* 'upper' to distinguish it from *Brodesideling* (Sydling St Nicholas).

Symondsbury *Simondesberge* 1086 (Domesday Book), *Simunisberge* 1212. 'Hill or barrow of a man called Sigemund', from an Old English personal name and *beorg*. The river here is now called Simene, a back-formation from Symondsbury.

Tadden (in Pamphill) probably *Tadhavene* 1327, 'haven or place of shelter for toads', from Old English *tāde* and *hæfen*. The name is perhaps jocular or may refer literally to the marshy ground here.

Tadnoll Dairy and Mill (in Chaldon Herring) *Tadenhole* 1281, *Tadynollesmyll* 1463. Probably 'toad-infested hollow', from Old English *tāde* (genitive singular *tādan* or plural *tādena*) and *hol*.

Talbot Village (in Bournemouth) district named c.1860 after the local landowners, the *Talbot* sisters.

Tarrant, River an old Celtic river-name, first recorded in 10th century, a variant of Trent, 'trespasser', i.e. 'river liable to floods'. The Tarrant gives its name to eight different parishes on its banks.

Tarrant Crawford *Tarente* 1086 (Domesday Book), *Little Craweford* 1280, *Tarrant Crawford or Little Crawford* 1795. Originally named from River Tarrant. *Little Crawford* to distinguish it from *Great Crawford* in Spetisbury on opposite bank of River Stour, 'crow ford', from Old English *crāwe* and *ford*.

Tarrant Gunville *Tarente* 1086 (Domesday Book), *Tarente Gundevill* 1233. 'Estate on River Tarrant held by the *Gundeville* family', here in the 12th and 13th centuries.

Tarrant Hinton *Terente* 877 (15th century copy of Saxon charter), *Tarente* 1086 (Domesday Book), *Tarente Hyneton* 1280. 'Estate on River Tarrant belonging to a religious community', Old English *hīwan* (genitive *hīgna*) and *tūn,* referring to Shaftesbury Abbey.

Tarrant Keynston *Tarente* 1086 (Domesday Book), *Tarente Kahaines* 1225, *Tarente Keyneston* 1303. 'Estate on River Tarrant held by the *Cahaignes* family', here from 12th to 14th century, with Old English *tūn* 'estate'.

Tarrant Launceston *Tarente* 1086 (Domesday Book), *Tarente Loueweniston* 1280. 'Estate on River Tarrant held by a man called *Lēofwine* or a family called *Lowin*', with Old English *tūn* 'estate'.

Tarrant Monkton *Tarente* 1086 (Domesday Book), *Tarenta Monachorum* 12th century, *Tarent Moneketon* 1280. 'Estate on River Tarrant belonging to the monks', from Old English *munuc* and *tūn,* with reference to the possession of this manor by the priory of Cranborne and the abbey of Tewkesbury. Latin *Monachorum,* 'of the monks' found up to 1556.

Tarrant Rawston *Tarente* 1086 (Domesday Book), *Tarente Antyoche* 1288, *Tarrant Rawston alias Antyocke* 1535. The earlier name, 'estate on River Tarrant held by the *Antioch* family', was in use until the 16th century; this family held the manor in the 13th and 14th centuries. The later addition *Rawston* probably means 'Ralph's estate', from Old English *tūn* 'manor, estate'.

Tarrant Rushton *Tarente* 1086 (Domesday Book), *Tarente Russeus* 1280, *Tarente Russcheweston* 1307. 'Estate (Old English *tūn*) on River Tarrant held by the *de Rusceaus* family'; this family held the manor in the 13th century. In medieval times sometimes *Tarente Vilers,* from the lords of the manor in the 12th century.

Tatton Farm and House (in Chickerell) *Tatetun, Tatentone* 1086 (Domesday Book), *Tattun* 1212. 'Farm of a man called Tata', from an Old English personal name and *tūn.*

Terrace Farm (in Stour Provost) 'Terrace' is a folk etymology of 'Terry's', found in *Terryeslane* 1420, *Tyrryestherne, Tarryescrofte* 1439, all named from a family called *Terry,* with Old English *lane* 'lane', *thyrne* 'thorn bush' and *croft* 'small enclosed field'.

Thickthorn Down (in Long Crichel) first recorded 1791.

Thorncombe (parish) *Tornecoma* 1086 (Domesday Book), *Thorncumbe* 1236. 'Valley where thorn-trees grow', from Old English *thorn* and *cumb.* This parish was in Devon until 1844.

Thorney Down Farm (in Sixpenny Handley) *la Thorne(y)downe* 1503, 1575. 'Hill or down growing with thorn-trees'.

Thornford *Thornford* 951 (12th century copy of Saxon charter), *Torneford*

1086 (Domesday Book), *Thorneford* 1249. 'Ford where thorn-trees grow', from Old English *thorn* and *ford*.

Thorngrove (in Gillingham) *Thorngraue* 1292, *Thorngroue* 1301. 'Thorn-tree copse', from Old English *thorn* and *grāf*. Also known as Queen's Farm in 18th century, no doubt referring to one of the English Queens who once possessed the manor of Gillingham.

Thornhill, 'hill where thorn-trees grow', from Old English *thorn* and *hyll*: (i) **Thornhill** (in Stalbridge) *Thornhill* 1244. (ii) **Thornhill Farm** (in Broadwey) *Thornhulle* 1431. (iii) **Thorn Hill Farm** (in Holt) *Tornehelle* 1086 (Domesday Book), *Thornhill* 1212.

Thornicombe (in Blandford St Mary) *Tornecome* 1086 (Domesday Book). 'Thorn-tree valley', from Old English *thorn* and *cumb*.

Thorton Farm (in Marnhull) *Thorntune* 958 (15th century copy of Saxon charter), *Torentone* 1086 (Domesday Book). 'Thorn-tree farm', or 'thorn enclosure', from Old English *thorn* and *tūn*.

Three Legged Cross (in Verwood) recorded from 16th century, perhaps with reference to a T-junction (with *cross* meaning cross-roads) or to a gallows (which was nicknamed *three legged mare*).

Throop, from Old English *throp* 'an outlying farm or secondary settlement': (i) **Throop** (in Bournemouth) *la Throup* 12th century. (ii) **Throop** (in Turners Puddle) *la Trop* 1237, *Thrope* 1268. (iii) **Throop Dairy House** (in Maiden Newton) *la Thrope* 1268.

Thurnwood Farm (in Mappowder) *Thurnwodd* 1567. 'Thorn-bush wood', from Old English *thyrne* and *wudu*.

Tiley (in Buckland Newton) *Tylly* 1244, *Tyleye* 1299. 'Wood or clearing where tiles are made', from Old English *tigel* and *lēah*.

Tilly Whim Caves (in Swanage) name for remains of ancient stone quarry not recorded before 1811, probably from the Dorset surname *Tilly* with the word *whim* 'a windlass, a winding gear'.

Tincleton *Tincladene* 1086 (Domesday Book), *Tyncleden* 1268. Probably 'valley of the small farms', from Old English *tȳnincel* and *denu*. The alteration of the ending -*den* to -*ton* is relatively recent.

Todber *Todeberie* 1086 (Domesday Book), *Totebera* 1194. Probably 'hill or grove of a man called Tota', from Old English *beorg* or *bearu* and an Old English personal name. However the first element may be Old English *tōte* 'a look-out'.

Tollard Farnham (in Farnham) *Toulard Fernham* 1282. This part of Farnham was held in the 13th century by the family of Brian *de Tollard* (from neighbouring parish of Tollard Royal in Wiltshire),

Tollerford (in Frome Vauchurch) *Tolreforde* 1086. 'Ford over River

Toller', from Old English *ford*. Toller, the original name of River Hooke, is probably an old Celtic river-name meaning 'hollow stream, stream running in a deep valley'. See Hooke.

Toller Fratrum and Toller Porcorum *Tolre* 1086 (Domesday Book), *Tolre Fratrum, Tolre Porcorum* 1340. Named from River *Toller,* now called Hooke, see Tollerford. The two Latin additions are humorously contrasting, *Fratrum* meaning 'of the brethren' because this manor once belonged to the Knights Hospitallers, *Porcorum* meaning 'of the pigs' from its herds of swine! In fact Toller Porcorum is usually *Swyne Tolre* in early records.

Toller Whelme (in Corscombe) *Tollor aewylman* 1035 (12th century copy of Saxon charter), *Tolre* 1086 (Domesday Book), *Tollre Euulme* 1268. 'Source of River Toller', from Old English *æwielm* 'river-spring'. For river-name, see Tollerford.

Tolpuddle *Pidele* 1086 (Domesday Book), *Tollepidele* 1210. 'Estate on River Piddle of a woman called Tola'. The Danish widow of King Edward the Confessor's housecarl, Tola gave all her lands including Tolpuddle to Abbotsbury abbey before 1066.

Totnell (in Leigh) *Totenhulle* 1327. 'Look-out hill', Old English *tōte* and *hyll,* or 'Tota's hill' from an Old English personal name.

Tout Hill (in East Stoke) 'look-out hill', from Old English *tōt-hyll.*

Townsend (in Bournemouth) *Tounesende* 1300. Self-explanatory, with reference to the south end of Holdenhurst.

Trent *Trente* 1086 (Domesday Book). Originally the name of the stream here (now called Trent Brook), an old Celtic river-name possibly originally meaning 'trespasser', i.e. 'river liable to floods'.

Trickett's Cross (in West Moors) *cross* 'cross-roads' and surname.

Trigon Farm and Hill (in Wareham) first recorded 1811, probably *trigon* 'triangle' describing shape of farm or hill.

Trill Bridge (in Fifehead Magdalen) probably named from *Trul* 1268 referring to small tributary of River Stour rising in Stour Provost. This stream-name has the same origin as the next name.

Trill Farm (in Beer Hackett) *Tril* 1012, *Trelle* 1086 (Domesday Book), *Trulle* 13th century. Named from the stream here, a tributary of River Yeo, from Old English *tyrl* 'the rolling or turning one'.

Troy Town Farm (in Puddletown) from *troy town* 'a maze'.

Tuckton (in Bournemouth) *Tuketon* 1248. 'Farm of a man called Tucca or Tocca', from an Old English personal name and *tūn.*

Turners Puddle *Pidele* 1086 (Domesday Book), *Tonerespydele* 1268. 'Estate on River Piddle held by the *Toner* family'; this family held the manor from the time of Domesday Book.

Turnworth *Torneworde* 1086 (Domesday Book), *Turnewurth* 1234. 'Thorn-bush enclosure, enclosure formed by thorn-bushes', from Old English *thyrne* and *worth*.

Tut Hill Farm (in Caundle Marsh) Old English *tōt-hyll* 'look-out hill'.

Twinwood Coppice (in Hinton St Mary) *Twynwood* 16th century. '(Land) between the woods', from Old English *betwēonan*.

Twofords Bridge (in Lydlinch) *bridge called Twyforde* 1496. See next name. Road to Sturminster Newton crosses two streams here.

Twyford (in Compton Abbas) *Tweyford* 1395. 'Double ford', from Old English *twī-* and *ford*. The road here crossed two streams, one called Twyford Brook, the other unnamed.

Tyneham *Tigeham* 1086 (Domesday Book), *Tynam* 1244. Probably 'goat's enclosure', Old English *tige* (genitive singular *tigan*) and *hamm*.

Uddens House (in Holt) *Udding* 956 (14th century copy of Saxon charter). Probably 'Udd(a)'s place', from an Old English masculine personal name *Udd* or *Udda* and *-ing*.

Ulwell (in Swanage) *Holewell* 1236, *Hulewlle* 1268. 'Spring or stream frequented by owls', from Old English *ūle* and *wella*.

Uploders (in Loders) *Lodre* 1086 (Domesday Book), *Uppelodres* 1445. See Loders; addition *Up* means 'higher upstream'.

Uppington (in Hinton Martell) *Uppington* 1838, probably '(land) higher up in the village', from Old English *upp, in*, and *tūn*.

Upton (in Lytchett Minster) *Upton* 1463, origin as next name.

Upton (in Osmington) *Upton* 1361. 'Higher farm', or 'higher part of the village', from Old English *upp* and *tūn*. Upton now lies in a valley, but the name must refer to the higher ground to the south.

Upwey *Wai(e)* 1086 (Domesday Book), *Uppeweie* 1241. 'Upper or higher manor on River Wey', Old English *upp*; the river rises here.

Vale Acre Farm (in Alderholt) *Vellak* 1314, *Fenlak* 1324. Probably 'fen stream', from Old English *fenn* and *lacu*, with Dorset dialect *V-* for *F-*, and *Vale* through folk etymology.

Vearse Farm (in Symondsbury) *Wotton Ver* 1304, *Vereswatton* 1371. The part of Watton held by the *Veer* family, here in 1304.

Venn Farm (in Stoke Abbott) *Venne* 1327. From Old English *fenn* 'fen, marshland', here with the old dialect pronunciation.

Verne Yeates (on Isle of Portland) *Ferne* 1321, *Fearne yates, Verne yates* 1608. Probably from Old English *fergen* 'mountain, wooded hill'; this is the highest part of the island, rising to nearly 500 feet. *Yeates* is from Old English *geat* 'gate, gap, pass'.

Verwood *Beuboys* 1288, *Fairwod* 1329. 'Beautiful wood', from Old English *fæger* and *wudu*, the modern form reflecting the Dorset dialect pronunciation with *V-* for *F-*. The 13th century spelling is from Old French *beu* and *bois*.

Waddock Farm (in Affpuddle) *Waddoke* 1564. Probably 'oak-tree near the ford', from Old English *wæd* and *āc*.

Waddon, Friar Waddon, Little Waddon (in Portesham) *Wadone* 1086 (Domesday Book), *Little Waddone* 1305, *Frerenwaddon* 1384. 'Hill or down where woad grows', from Old English *wād* and *dūn*. The addition *Friar* (earlier *Freren* 'of the Friars') refers to possession of lands here by the Knights Hospitallers. Friar Waddon is often called *Brodewaddon* ('broad Waddon') in medieval times.

Waddon Hill (in Loders) *Waddon* 1463. Origin as previous name.

Wadmill Farm (in Stour Provost) *Wabenhull* 1300. Probably 'hill of a man called Waba', from an Old English personal name and *hyll*. The recent alteration to *-mill* is due to folk etymology.

Wakeham (on Isle of Portland) *Wacombe* 1608. From Old English *cumb* 'valley', perhaps with Old English *wacu* 'a watch, a wake'.

Walditch (in Bothenhampton) *Waldic* 1086 (Domesday Book). 'Ditch with a wall or embankment', from Old English *weall* or *walu* and *dīc*.

Walford Bridge and Farm (in Wimborne Minster) *Walteford* 1086 (Domesday Book). Probably 'shaky, unsteady ford, i.e. ford difficult to cross', from Old English *wealt* and *ford*. The road from Cranborne into Wimborne crosses River Allen here.

Walkford (in Christchurch) *Walkeforde* 1280. Origin uncertain, perhaps 'ford where fulling takes place' or 'ford for walking across', from Middle English *walke*, but first element may be an old name *Wealce* ('the rolling one') of Walkford Brook, or an Old English personal name *Walca*.

Wall Farm (in Stoke Abbott) *Welle* 1251, *Walle* 1332. Old English *wella* 'spring' or *weall* 'wall.

Walton Elm (in Marnhull) *Walton* 13th century. Old English *tūn* 'estate', with *weald* 'woodland' or *weall* 'wall'. *Elm* from 1811.

Wantsley Farm (in Broadwindsor) *Wantesleghe* 1244. 'Clearing of a man called Want', from Old English personal name and *lēah*.

Wareham *Werham* 9th century (Anglo-Saxon Chronicle), *Warham* 1086 (Domesday Book). 'Homestead by a weir', from Old English *wer* or *wær* and *hām*. It lies on River Frome.

Warmwell *Warmewelle*, *Warmwelle* 1086 (Domesday Book), *Wermewelle* 1205. 'The warm spring', from Old English *wearm* and *wella*. There is a spring just north of the village.

Warren (in Bere Regis) *Warame* 1546, *Rabbit Warren* 1845. The game preserve (Middle English *wareine)* belonged to Tarrant abbey.

Warren Hill (in Bournemouth) *The Warren* in 17th century.

Watcombe Bottom (in Alton Pancras) *Whetecombe* 891 (14th century copy of Saxon charter). 'Valley where wheat is grown', from Old English *hwæte* and *cumb.*

Watercombe *Watrecome* 1086 (Domesday Book), *Watercumbe* 1204. 'Wet valley', from Old English *wæter* 'water' and *cumb.*

Waterloo Farm (in Gillingham) alluding to the famous battle of 1815.

Waterston (in Puddletown) *Pidere* 1086 (Domesday Book), *Walterton* 1227, *Pydele Waltereston* 1268. Originally named from River Piddle, later 'Walter's farm', from Old English *tūn.*

Watton (in Symondsbury) *Wutton* 1228, *Wottune* 1256. Probably 'farm on River Woth', from Old English *tūn. Woth* is the old name of River Brit, see Wooth Grange and also Vearse Farm.

Waytown (in Netherbury) *Wayetowne* 1626, 'hamlet by the way or road', from Middle English *weye* and *toun.*

Weathergrove (in Sandford Orcas) *wederangrafe* 938 (12th century copy of Saxon charter), *Weregrave* 1086 (Domesday Book), *Wedergraue* 1378. Probably 'grove of a man called Wedera', from an Old English personal name and *grāf.*

Week Common and Farm (in St Leonards and St Ives) *Wike* 1327, *Week* 1759. 'Specialized or dairy farm', Old English *wīc.*

Week Street Down (in Gussage St Michael) the stretch of the Salisbury to Blandford road flanked by the down is *wic herepath* in 935, 'highway to the farm', from Old English *wīc* and *here-pæth.*

Wellwood (in Beaminster) *Welle* 1086 (Domesday Book). Old English *wella* 'spring or stream', with the later addition of *wood.*

West Bay (in Bridport) a modern name.

Westbourne (in Bournemouth) like Northbourne and Southbourne, a name of recent invention for a district of the town.

Westbrook Farm (in Gillingham) *Westbrooke* 1609. Named from West Brook, a small tributary of the River Stour.

Westbrook House (in Upwey) *Westebroke* 1285. '(Place) to the west of the brook (River Wey)', from Old English *westan* and *brōc.*

Westbury Farm (in Tarrant Gunville) *Westbury* 1414. Middle English *bury* 'manor house', see Eastbury House in same parish.

Westcombe Coppice (in Hooke) *Westcombe* 1510, 'west valley'.

Westfields (in Mappowder) *Westfyldes* 1536, 'west fields'.

Westford Farm (in Thorncombe) *Westforde* 1291, 'west' in relation to the ford that gave name to Forde Abbey in this parish.

West Hall (in Folke) *Westhalle* 1352, from *hall* 'manor house'.

Westley Wood (in Sturminster Marshall) *Westleye* 1306. 'West wood or woodland glade', from Old English *west* and *lēah*.

West Moors *La More* 1310, *Moures* 1407, *West Moors* 1591. 'The marshy ground(s)', from Old English *mōr,* see East Moors Farm.

Weston (on Isle of Portland) *Westone* 1324. 'West farm or village', from Old English *west* and *tūn,* in contrast with Easton.

Westover Farm (in St Leonards and St Ives) *Westover* 1638. '(Place on) west river-bank (of Avon)', Old English *ōfer* 'bank'.

Westover Farm (in Wootton Fitzpaine) *Westouer* 1332. Identical in origin with the previous name.

Westport House (in Wareham) *Bywesteport* 1264. Probably '(place) to the west of the town', Old English *bī, westan* and *port*.

West Wood (in Ashmore) *Westewode* 1280, 'west wood'.

Westworth Farm (in Edmondsham) *Worth* 1268. Old English *worth* 'enclosure'; *west* from 18th century, see Eastworth Farm.

Wey, River see under Broadwey.

Weymouth *Waimouthe* 934 (later copy of Saxon charter), *Weymuth* 1248. 'Mouth of River Wey', from Old English *mūtha*.

Whatcombe, 'wet valley' or 'valley where wheat is grown', from Old English *wæt* or *hwæte* and *cumb*: (i) **Whatcombe** (in Winterborne Whitechurch) *W(h)atecumbe* 1288. In early times sometimes called *Winterborne Whatcombe* from its location on River Winterborne. (ii) **Whatcombe Down** (in Kingston Russell) *Whatecome* 1340.

Whatley Farm (in Beaminster) *Whatley* 1623, identical in origin with next name.

Whetley Farm (in Broadwindsor) *Hwatelegh* 13th century. 'Clearing where wheat is grown', Old English *hwæte* and *lēah*.

Whistley Farm (in Gillingham) not on record before the 19th century, from Old English *west* 'west' and *lēah* 'wood, clearing' .

Whitchurch Canonicorum *Witcerce* 1086 (Domesday Book), *Witechurch* 1231, *Whytchyrche* 1242, *Whitchurch Canonicorum* 1262. 'White church', that is probably 'stone-built church', from Old English *hwīt* and *cirice*. The Latin addition *Canonicorum* means 'of the canons (of Salisbury)'. Church dedication to Candida (St Wite) may be derived from the place-name rather than vice versa.

Whitcombe *Widecome* 934 (later copy of Saxon charter), *Widecome* 1086 (Domesday Book). 'Wide valley', from Old English *wīd* and *cumb*.

Whitecliff Farm (in Swanage) *Witeclive* 1086 (Domesday Book),

Whyteclive 1251. '(Place at) the white cliff, from Old English *hwīt* and *clif*, with reference to the chalk cliff near here.

Whitefield (in Morden) *Whytewell* 1422. 'White spring or stream', from Old English *hwīt* and *wella*.

White Lackington (in Piddletrenthide) *Wyghtlakynton* 1354. 'Farm called after a man named Wihtlāc', OE *-ingtūn* and personal name.

White Mead (in Puddletown) *la Wytemede* 1270. 'White meadow'.

White Mill (in Shapwick) *Wytemull* 1341. Self-explanatory, from Old English *hwīt* and *myln*. It gives name to White Mill Bridge in Sturminster Marshall.

White Nothe (in Owermoigne) *the White North* 1649. Old English *hwīt* 'white' (referring to chalk cliffs) and *hnoth* 'knoll or hill'.

White Sheet Hill (in Holt) *White Shite Heth* 1547. Probably Old English *scyte* '(steep) slope or hill', with *hwīt* 'white' (alluding to soil colour) and (earlier) *hæth* 'heath'.

Whiteway, 'white (chalky) way', from Old English *hwīt* and *weg*: (i) **Whiteway** (in Tyneham) *Whitewey* 1327. (ii) **Whiteway Farm** (in Church Knowle) *Wyteweye* 1284. (iii) **Whitey Top** (in Pentridge) named from *Whiteway* 1838.

Whitfield Farm (in Bradford Peverell) *Whitewell* 1195, *Witewell* 1201, *Whytewelle* 1300. 'White (chalky) spring', from Old English *hwīt* and *wella*. Modern alteration of the name to *-field* is due to confusion with Frome Whitfield to which manor it once belonged.

Whitfield Farm (in Lillington) *Whitefeld* 1309. Apparently self-explanatory, from Old English *hwīt* and *feld*, but probably signifying 'unwooded open country, dry open pasture'.

Wick (in Bournemouth) *la Wych* 12th century, *Wyke* 1263. 'The specialized farm or dairy farm', from Old English *wīc*.

Wigbeth (in Horton) first recorded 1840, origin uncertain.

Wilkswood Farm (in Langton Matravers) *Wilceswde, Wilchesode* 1086 (Domesday Book), *Wylcheswode* 1305. Probably 'wood of a man called Willic', from an Old English personal name and *wudu*.

Wilksworth Farm (in Colehill) *Wedechesworde* 1086 (Domesday Book), *Wudekesworth* 1244. Probably 'enclosure of a man called Wuduc', from an Old English personal name and *worth*.

Wimborne Minster *Winburnan* 9th century (Anglo-Saxon Chronicle), *Winburne* 1086 (Domesday Book), *Wymburneminstre* 1236. 'Meadow stream', from Old English *winn* and *burna*, originally the name of River Allen. *Minster* is from Old English *mynster* '(the church of) a monastery', referring to the nunnery founded here by Queen Cūthburh of Wessex in the early 8th century.

Wimborne St Giles *Winburne* 1086 (Domesday Book), *Vpwymburn Sancti Egidij* 1268, *Upwymbourne St Giles* 1399. Like Wimborne Minster, named from the river here, now called Allen. *Up* means 'higher up (the river)', *St Giles* (Latin *Egidius*) is from the dedication of the church. In early times also *Upwymburne Malemayns* or *Pleycy*, from two families here in the 13th century.

Winfrith Newburgh *Winfrode* 1086 (Domesday Book), *Wynifred Neuburgh* 1288. An old Celtic river-name, meaning 'white or bright stream', from *winn* and *frud*, originally the name of River Win, a tributary of River Frome. *Newburgh* is the name of the family who held the manor from the 12th century onwards.

Winkton (in Christchurch) *Weringetone* 1086 (Domesday Book), *Wineketon* 1236. 'Farm of a man called Wineca', from an Old English personal name and *tūn*.

Winspit (in Worth Matravers) first recorded 1786, possibly an old name meaning 'stone pit with a winch', from Old English *wince.*

Winterborne, River there are two rivers so called in Dorset, each giving name to several villages. The South Winterborne is a tributary of River Frome, the more northerly Winterborne is a tributary of River Stour. 'Winter stream', that is one that flows most strongly in winter, from Old English *winter-burna.*

Winterborne Came *Wintreburne* 1086 (Domesday Book), *Winterburn Caam* 1280. One of the several places named from the South Winterborne river. The addition *Came* is from the possession of this manor by the abbey of St Stephen at *Caen* (in Normandy) from the time of William the Conqueror.

Winterborne Clenston *Wintreburne* 1086 (Domesday Book), *Winterborn Clench* 1243, *Clenchton* 1268, *Wynterburn Clencheston* 1303. 'Estate on River Winterborne held by the *Clench* family', here from the 13th century, from Old English *tūn.*

Winterborne Herringston *Wintreburne* 1086 (Domesday Book), *Winterborn Harang* 1243, *Wynterburne Heringeston* 1288. Named from the same river as Winterborne Came. Addition is from the family of *Harang*, here from the 13th century, with Old English *tūn* 'estate'. For the same family, see Chaldon and Langton Herring.

Winterborne Houghton *Wintreburne* 1086 (Domesday Book), *Wynterburn Hugheton* 1288. 'Estate on the River Winterborne held by Hugh', with Old English *tūn* 'manor, estate'. One *Hugh de Boscherbert* held a manor here at the time of Domesday Book.

Winterborne Kingston *Wintreburne* 1086 (Domesday Book), *Kingeswinterburn* 1194. Named from the same river as Winterborne Clenston. Kingston is 'king's estate', from Old English *tūn*; it was held by the king from the time of King John.

Winterborne Monkton *Wintreburne* 1086 (Domesday Book), *Wynterburn Moneketon* 1268. Named from the same river as Winterborne Came. *Monkton* means 'estate or village of the monks', from Old English *munuc* and *tūn*, since this place belonged to the Cluniac priory of Le Wast near Boulogne from the early 13th century. In medieval times often *Winterborne West*.

Winterborne Muston (in Winterborne Kingston) *Wintreburne* 1086 (Domesday Book), *Winterborn Musters* 1243, *Winterborne Mousterston* 1310. Named from the same river as Winterborne Clenston. *Muston* means 'estate of the *de Musters* family', from Old English *tūn*; this family was here from the 13th century, see also Muston. In medieval times known as *Winterborne Turberville*, from the *Turberville* family who also had lands here.

Winterborne St Martin *Wintreburne* 1086 (Domesday Book), *Wynterburn Sancti Martini* 1244, *Wynterburn Seynt Martyn* 1280. Named from the same river as Winterborne Came. 'St Martin' is from the dedication of the church. Martinstown is an alternative modern name, first found at the end of the 15th century.

Winterborne Stickland *Winterburne* 1086 (Domesday Book), *Winterburn Stikellane* 1203. 'Estate on River Winterborne with a steep lane', from Old English *sticol* and *lane*. Lanes climb the hills to east and west out of the deep valley in which the village lies. The word *stickle* 'steep' survives in Dorset dialect.

Winterborne Tomson *Winterburne* 942 (15th century copy of Saxon charter), *Wintreburne* 1086 (Domesday Book), *Winterborn Thom'* 1243, *Wynterbourn Thomaston* 1280. 'Estate on the River Winterborne held by someone called Thomas', from Old English *tūn* 'manor, estate'.

Winterborne Whitechurch *Wintreburne* 1086 (Domesday Book), *Winterburn Albi Monasterii* 1201, *Winterburn Blancmustier* 1212, *Wynterborn Wytecherch* 1268. 'Estate on the River Winterborne with a white (perhaps stone-built) church', from Old English *hwīt* and *cirice* (alternating with Latin *albus* and *monasterium* and Old French *blanc* and *moustier* in early spellings).

Winterborne Zelstone *Wintreborne* 1086 (Domesday Book), *Wynterburne Malreward* 1230, *Wynterbourn Selyston* 1350. Named from the more northerly River Winterborne. Earlier affix from *Malreward* family, here from 12th to 16th centuries (see Kingston Maurward). Later affix from family called *de Seles*, with Old English *tūn* 'estate'.

Winterbourne Abbas *Winceburnan* 987 (13th century copy of Saxon charter), *Wintreburne* 1086 (Domesday Book), *Wynterburn Abbatis* 1244. Named from same river as Winterbome Came. Latin *abbas* 'abbot' from early possession by Cerne Abbey. In medieval times sometimes known as *Watreleswyntreburn*, 'waterless' because of dryness of South Winterborne river here in some seasons.

Winterbourne Steepleton *Wintreburne* 1086 (Domesday Book), *Stipelwinterburn* 1199, *Wynterburn Stepilton* 1244. Named from the same river as Winterborne Came. Steepleton means 'village with a church tower or steeple', from Old English *stīepel* and *tūn*.

Winterhays (in Yetminster) *Wynterhey* 1327. 'Enclosure used in winter', from Old English *winter* and *hæg*.

Winton (in Bournemouth) district named from Earl of Eglinton created also Earl of *Winton* in 1859, a kinsman of the Talbot sisters, see Talbot Village.

Witchampton *Wichemetune* 1086 (Domesday Book), *Wichamton* 1216. Probably 'farm of the dwellers at a place called *Wīchām*', that is at 'a village associated with a Romano-British settlement', from Old English *wīc, hæme, tūn*. There are Roman remains here.

Withyhook Mill (in Leigh) *Widihoc* 1197, *la Wytheoc* 1283. 'Spit of land growing with willows', from Old English *wīthig* and *hōc*.

Wolfeton (in Charminster) *Wolueton* 1231. 'Farm of a man called Wulfa', from an Old English personal name and *tūn*.

Wolfridge Farm (in Motcombe) probably *Welrigge* 1292, 'ridge where there is a spring or stream', from Old English *wella* and *hrycg,* perhaps with reference to the higher ground to the east. *Wolf-* in the modern form is due to folk etymology.

Wonston (in Hazelbury Bryan) *Wolmerston* 1280. 'Farm of a man called Wulfmær', from an Old English personal name and *tūn*.

Woodbridge, 'wooden bridge', from Old English *wudu* and *brycg*: (i) **Woodbridge** (in Fontmell Magna) *wde bricge* 932, *Wodebrygge* 1395. (ii) **Woodbridge** (in Holwell) *Wudebrige* 1194.

Woodbury Hill (in Bere Regis) *Wudebur* 1254, *Wodeburi* 1287, *Wodebery hill* 1476. 'Fortification by the wood', from Old English *wudu* and *burh*. There are remains of an earthwork here.

Woodcutts, 'cottages in a wood', from Old English *wudu* and *cot*: (i) **Woodcutts** (in Sixpenny Handley) *Wodecote* 1244, *Wodecotys* 1456. (ii) **Woodcutts Farm** (in Hinton Martell) *la Wodecote* 1290.

Woodhouse Cross (in Gillingham) *Woodhowse Crosse* 1609. 'House in the wood', or 'house made of wood', with *cross* 'cross-roads'.

Woodlake (in Bloxworth) first recorded in the 17th century. 'Woodland stream', from Old English *wudu* and *lacu*.

Woodlands *Wodelande* 1244. 'Wooded estate or tract of land', or 'land cleared for cultivation near or within a wood', from Old English *wudu* and *land*. The final *-s* in the name, representing a plural form, only appears in the 18th century.

Woodrow, 'row of trees, narrow wood', from Old English *wudu* and *rāw*: (i) **Woodrow** (in Fifehead Neville) *Woderove* 14th century. (ii) **Woodrow** (in Hazelbury Bryan) *Woodrowe* 1580. (iii) **Woodrow Farms** (in Stourton Caundle) *Woderewe* 1327.

Woodsford *Werdesford, Wardesford* 1086 (Domesday Book), *Wyrdesford,* 1280. 'Ford of a man called Weard', Old English personal name and *ford*.

Woodstreet Farm (in Wool) *Windestorte* 1086 (Domesday Book, for *Wiude-*), *Wudestort, Wodestort* 1234. 'Tail of land by a wood', from Old English *wudu* and *steort*.

Woodville (in Stour Provost) *Wodefeld* 1444. 'Wood field'.

Woodyates, East and West (in Pentridge) *Wdegeate, Wudegate* 9th century, *Odiete* 1086 (Domesday Book), *Wudiete* 1199. '(Place at) the gate or gap in the wood', from Old English *wudu* and *geat*. The gate or gap may have been at Bokerly Junction, where Bokerly Ditch was breached by the road from Blandford Forum to Salisbury. Final *-s*, a plural form, only appears in the 16th century.

Wool *Wille, Welle* 1086 (Domesday Book), *Welles* 1166, *Woll* 1249. '(Place at) the spring or springs', from Old English *wella*. There are several springs south of the village. This name preserves the genuine West Saxon dialect form of the word *well*.

Wool Bridge, Woolbridge Heath (in East Stoke) *Wullebrigg* 1244, *Wollebrigge* 1343. 'The bridge near Wool', from Old English *brycg*. This is an important crossing of River Frome.

Woolcombe, 'valley with a spring or stream', from Old English *wella* and *cumb*: (i) **Woolcombe** (in Melbury Bubb) *Wellecome* 1086 (Domesday Book), *Wulecumb* 1219. (ii) **Woolcombe Farm** (in Toller Porcorum) *Wellacome, Wilecome* 1086 (Domesday Book), *Wollecumbe* 1285.

Woolgarston (in Corfe Castle) *Orgarestone* 1086 (Domesday Book), *Wulgareston* 1213. 'Farm of a man called Wulfgār', from an Old English personal name and *tūn*.

Woolland *Wennland* 833, *Winlande* 1086 (Domesday Book), *Wuland*

1212. 'Estate, or cultivated land, consisting largely of meadow', from Old English *wynn* and *land*.

Wools Bridge, Woolsbridge (in Verwood) *Woolles bridge* 1618. Probably Old English *wella* 'stream' (referring to Moors River).

Wooth Grange (in Netherbury) originally *Woth Fraunceys* 1276. *Woth* is the old name of the River Brit and probably meant 'sound, melody'. An estate here was held by a family called *Fraunceys*.

Wootton Fitzpaine *Wodetone, Odetun* 1086 (Domesday Book), *Wotton Fitz Payn* 1392. 'Farm in or by a wood', from Old English *wudu* and *tūn*. Manorial affix from *Fitz Payn* family, as in Okeford Fitzpaine.

Wootton Glanville see Glanvilles Wootton.

Wootton North *Wotton* 1180, *Wuttun* 1226. Identical in origin with Wootton Fitzpaine; 'north' in relation to Glanvilles Wootton.

Worbarrow (Bay and Tout) (in Tyneham) *Wyrebarowe* 1462, *Warbarrow Tout* 1841. Probably 'hill where watch was kept', from Old English *weard* and *beorg*, with reference to the conical hill here (Old English *tōte* 'lookout hill') which provides good views to east and west along the coast.

Worgret (in Arne) *Vergroh, Weregrote* 1086 (Domesday Book), *Wergerod* 1202. 'Gallows for criminals', from Old English *wearg-rōd*. Worgret is a mile from Wareham on the Dorchester road.

Worth Matravers *Orde, Wirde* 1086 (Domesday Book), *Wurthe* 1220, *Worth Matrauers* 1664. 'The enclosure', Old English *worth*. Manorial affix from *Mautravers* family, here in 14th century.

Wrackleford House (in Stratton) *Wrakylford* 1544. 'Ford of a man called Wræcwulf', from an Old English personal name and *ford*.

Wraxall *Brocheshale* 1086 (Domesday Book, for *Wroches-*), *Wrokeshal* 1196. 'Nook of land or hollow frequented by the buzzard or other bird of prey', from Old English *wrocc* and *healh*.

Wych (in Bothenhampton) *la Wiche* 1481. From Old English *wīc* 'dairy farm', or *wice* 'wych-elm'.

Wyke, 'the dwelling, the specialized farm or dairy farm', from Old English *wīc*: (i) **Wyke Farm** (in Castleton) *Wica* 1125. (ii) **Wyke Farm and Down** (in Gussage All Saints) *Wyke* 1276. (iii) **Wyke Farm** (in Halstock) *Wika* 1236. (iv) **Wyke Marsh** (in Gillingham) named from *Wyke* 1244. (v) **Wyke Oliver House** (near Preston) *Wyke* 1327, *Weeke Oliver* 1616. John *Oliver* held lands here in 1640. (vi) **Wyke Wood** (in Abbotsbury) *Wike* 1269, *Wyke Wodde* 1495.

Wyke Regis *Wike* 984, *Wick* 1220, *Kingeswik* 1242, *Wyke Regis* 1407. In this name the Old English word *wīc* may have the meaning 'specialized farm' or 'harbour, fishery'. It was anciently royal demesne, hence the

Latin addition *Regis* 'of the king'.

Wyld Farms, Monkton Wyld (in Wootton Fitzpaine) *La Wilæ* 1189, *Wila* 1204, *Monkynwyll* 1535. From Old English *wīl* 'wile, trick', probably here 'trap or snare'. The spelling with *-d* is quite a recent development. *Monkyn-*, later altered to Monkton, means 'of the monks', alluding to possession of lands here by Forde Abbey.

Wynford Eagle *Wenfrot* 1086 (Domesday Book), *Winfrot Gileberti de Aquila* 1204, *Wynford Aquile* 1275, *Wynfrod Egle* 1288. An old Celtic name for the stream on which Wynford stands, identical in origin with Winfrith. Manorial addition from the family of *del Egle* (latinized as *de Aquila*) from Laigle in France.

Wytch Farm and Heath (in Corfe Castle) *Wicha* 12th century, *Wyche* 1498. Named from River Wych, now called Corfe River, although its estuary in Poole Harbour is still known as Wych Channel. From Old English *wice* 'wych-elm'.

Wytherstone Farm (in Powerstock) *Wytherston* 1258, *Wytheston* 1269. 'Farm of a man called Wither', Old English personal name and *tūn*, or 'stone near which willows grow', Old English *wīthig* and *stān*.

Yard Dairy (in Rampisham) *Le Yerde* 13th century. From Old English *gierd* 'a measure of land consisting of about thirty acres'.

Yardgrove Farm (in Marnhull) *Gerdegrave* 1258, *Yerdgrave* 1270. Probably 'grove or copse where rods or spars are obtained', from Old English *gerd* and *grāf*.

Yellowham Hill and Wood (in Puddletown) *Golwham* 1270, *Yolweham* 1404. 'Yellow enclosure', from Old English *geolu* and *hamm*. 'Yellow' may allude to the soil or to yellow flowers.

Yetminster *Etiminstre* 1086 (Domesday Book), *Yateminstre* 1226. 'Church of a man called Ēata', from an Old English personal name and *mynster*. He perhaps founded or endowed the church.

Yewstock (in Hinton St Mary) *la Hevedstocke* 1340. 'The head post', i.e. 'the post on which the head of a criminal was exposed', from Old English *hēafod-stocc*. The cottage of this name stands on the parish boundary.

Yondover (in Loders) *Endouer* 1454, *Yendover* 1544. '(Land) beyond the river-bank', from Old English *begeondan* and *ōfer*.

The

DISCOVER DORSET

Series of Books

A series of paperback books providing informative illustrated
introductions to Dorset's history, culture and way of life.
The following titles have so far been published.

BLACKMORE VALE *Hilary Townsend*
BRIDGES *David McFetrich and Jo Parsons*
CASTLES AND FORTS *Colin Pomeroy* COAST & SEA *Sarah Welton*
CRANBORNE CHASE *Desmond Hawkins*
DOWNS, MEADOWS & PASTURES *Jim White*
DRESS AND TEXTILES *Rachel Worth* FARMING *J.H. Bettey*
FARMHOUSES & COTTAGES *Michael Billett*
FOLLIES *Jonathan Holt* FOSSILS *Richard Edmonds*
GEOLOGY *Paul Ensom* THE GEORGIANS *Jo Draper*
HEATHLANDS *Lesley Haskins* THE INDUSTRIAL PAST *Peter Stanier*
ISLE OF PURBECK *Paul Hyland* LEGENDS *Jeremy Harte*
LOST VILLAGES *Linda Viner* MILLS *Peter Stanier*
PLACE-NAMES *A.D. Mills* PORTLAND *Stuart Morris*
POTTERY *Penny Copland-Griffiths* THE PREHISTORIC AGE *Bill Putnam*
RAILWAY STATIONS *Mike Oakley* REGENCY, RIOT & REFORM *Jo Draper*
RIVERS & STREAMS *John Wright*
ROADS, TRACKS & TURNPIKES *David Viner*
THE ROMANS *Bill Putnam* SAXONS & VIKINGS *David Hinton*
SHIPWRECKS *Maureen Attwooll* STONE QUARRYING *Jo Thomas*
TOWNS *John Porter* TUDORS & STUARTS *J.H. Bettey*
THE VICTORIANS *Jude James* WOODLANDS *Anne Horsfall*

All the books about Dorset published by The Dovecote Press
are available in bookshops throughout the county,
or in case of difficulty direct from the publishers.
The Dovecote Press Ltd, Stanbridge, Wimborne Minster, Dorset BH21 4JD
Tel: 01258 840549 www.dovecotepress.com